GOD'S WORD THROUGH PREACHING: THE LYMAN BEECHER LECTURES BEFORE THE THEOLOGICAL DEPARTMENT OF YALE COLLEGE. (FOURTH SERIES), PP. 7-273

Published @ 2017 Trieste Publishing Pty Ltd

ISBN 9780649594726

God's Word Through Preaching: The Lyman Beecher Lectures Before the Theological Department of Yale College. (Fourth Series), pp. 7-273 by John Hall

Except for use in any review, the reproduction or utilisation of this work in whole or in part in any form by any electronic, mechanical or other means, now known or hereafter invented, including xerography, photocopying and recording, or in any information storage or retrieval system, is forbidden without the permission of the publisher, Trieste Publishing Pty Ltd, PO Box 1576 Collingwood, Victoria 3066 Australia.

All rights reserved.

Edited by Trieste Publishing Pty Ltd.
Cover @ 2017

This book is sold subject to the condition that it shall not, by way of trade or otherwise, be lent, re-sold, hired out, or otherwise circulated without the publisher's prior consent in any form or binding or cover other than that in which it is published and without a similar condition including this condition being imposed on the subsequent purchaser.

www.triestepublishing.com

JOHN HALL

GOD'S WORD THROUGH PREACHING: THE LYMAN BEECHER LECTURES BEFORE THE THEOLOGICAL DEPARTMENT OF YALE COLLEGE. (FOURTH SERIES), PP. 7-273

JOHN HALL

GOD'S WORD THROUGH PREACHING;
THE LYMAN BEECHER LECTURES
BEFORE THE THEOLOGICAL
DEPARTMENT OF YALE COLLEGE.
(FOURTH SERIES), PP. 7-273

Trieste

GOD'S WORD

THROUGH PREACHING.

THE LYMAN BEECHER LECTURES BEFORE

THE THEOLOGICAL DEPARTMENT

OF YALE COLLEGE.

(FOURTH SERIES.)

BY

JOHN HALL, D.D.

NEW YORK:
DODD & MEAD, PUBLISHERS,
751 Broadway.

Copyright, Dodd & Mead, 1875.

FROM THE RECORDS OF THE CORPORATION OF YALE COLLEGE,
APRIL 12, 1871.

"Voted to accept the offer of Mr. Henry W. Sage, of New York City, of the sum of ten thousand dollars for the founding of a lectureship in the Theological Department, on a branch of Pastoral Theology, to be designated 'The Lyman Beecher Lectureship on Preaching,' to be filled from time to time, upon the appointment of this Corporation, by a minister of the gospel, of any evangelical denomination, who has been markedly successful in the special work of the Christian ministry."

YALE COLLEGE, THEOLOGICAL DEPARTMENT,
March 11, 1875.

REV. JOHN HALL, D.D.:

Dear Sir:—Allow us to thank you in our own behalf, and in behalf of the Theological Seminary under our care, for the course of lectures which you have just completed. The Lyman-Beecher Lectureship on Preaching will be of inestimable value to the churches, if, year after year, it shall continue to bear such fruit.

You have seen the close and delighted attention with which our students, and not a few others—most of them working ministers of the Gospel—have listened to these lectures. You have been giving—in your own style, simple, lucid, and forcible

—not a theory or science of Homiletics deduced from your study of great preachers, ancient and modern, but (in accordance with the intention of the generous founder) practical counsels, drawn from your own experience through a long and eminently successful ministry begun in your native country, and continued with undiminished fidelity in ours which has adopted you. We are sure that these young men, dispersed as they will soon be over the breadth of the continent, and some of them into other lands, will be better ministers, both in the pulpit and out of it, for what they have heard from you—better in the highest sense, for what we have valued most of all in these lectures is the deep and healthy religious impression which they have left upon the hearers.

We are happy to learn that the lectures are soon to be published, and we are confident that the ministry generally, of all denominations, and especially young ministers, will thank God for the grace that has been given to you for this good work.

We are, with much respect and affection, your brethren in the Gospel,

LEONARD BACON,
GEORGE E. DAY,
SAMUEL HARRIS,
JAMES M. HOPPIN,
GEORGE P. FISHER,
TIMOTHY DWIGHT.

LECTURE I.

IN entering on this course of lectures, Gentlemen, I feel bound to declare to you that my own judgment has been overruled, and that no one can have so strong a conviction of my inadequacy to this task at the close, as I have at the commencement. Nor did I labor to persuade myself of my unfitness in order to evade some labor, and, least of all, in order to escape an undesirable association. On the contrary, I was much touched by the practical catholicity of the Faculty of this Seminary in seeking out a comparative stranger, and one outside of that honored band whose education, intelligence, courage, and Christian worth, have made New England what it is, and stamped a New England impress on so much of America. But no eagerness to respond to this attractive overture blinded me to the truth, that all I know on this matter of preaching could be put into one lecture. Certain brethren, however, to whose views I could not but attach weight, assured me that the general subject of pulpit ministrations fairly came within the scope of the foundation, and that I was not expected to revolve in the same orbit, nor to shine with the same brilliancy as my predecessor; that, in fact—though they did not so phrase it—one like myself, a long way on this side of the extraordinary, might be an encouraging teacher and example to ordinary men, and, in detailing how commonplace qualities could be turned, by God's blessing on ordinary industry, to fair account, might guide, stimulate, and help students in theology. This last consideration, I confess, had the most weight with me. No talent is too great, no genius is too brilliant, no attainments are too rich, for the work of preaching; but, thank God, average capacity can be trained into such an instrument as God the Holy Ghost will employ for the " work of the ministry, for the edifying of the body of Christ." *

Preaching is not to be regarded and studied by itself, but in its relation to the whole work of the ministry. Nor is the ministry to be judged of as a detached piece of machinery, but in its place in the Church; and, once more, our notions of the ministry

---

* Eph. iv. 12.

and of preaching will be much modified by our conception of the Church's history, nature, objects, and powers. To offer a concise statement of these will occupy this opening hour, and it is hoped usefully introduce what is to be further presented.

The Church of God—in whose ministry, Gentlemen, you hope to serve—may be regarded in one of two aspects, when we speak of its history. We may think of it as one continuous body from the first family down to our own time, and to the end of the world, the same in substance throughout, though under diverse forms and dispensations. In this sense the Christian Church is not a new thing, but a development of what went before, the growth of a tree planted in Paradise. Israel was at one time "the Church in the Wilderness." * If we wished to furnish a history of the American nation, we might properly begin, like Bancroft, with Colonization, and different forms of administration and possession, entire or partial, by Dutch, French, English, until there came to be an independent people—yokes of bondage and elements of restriction being thrown off—and the community entered on an era of equal rela-

---

* Acts vii. 38.

tions with all the nations of the earth, free to all, free from all.

In this wide and comprehensive sense, the Church is the body of Christ.* For this Church which He loved, He gave Himself.† Much aid may be gained, then, in our inquiry, from knowing what manner of ministry God gave His Church, even in the earliest dispensations. The Church is one.

Or, we may speak of the Church as beginning with the appearance, or the ascension, or the gift of the Holy Ghost, or some other part of the work of our blessed Lord, after which it took the Christian name, and assumed, in the progress of events, new and appropriate form. So a historian of the United States might choose to commence his work with the Revolutionary War, or the proclamation of Independence. On this plan the writer would find himself obliged to make very full references to previous forces and conditions that formed the new national life; and precisely so, when we deal with the Christian Church *as such*, we cannot ignore, but are forced to dwell upon the character and influence of former dispensations as giving language and form to the Church of the Christian era.

---

* Col. i. 18. † Eph. v. 25.

Unless, indeed, we are concerned in controversies regarding the future, and anxious to find a basis for special interpretations, the date from which we reckon the history of the Church is of little practical importance.*

But this Church, in either aspect of it, is a divine institution. It is voluntary, indeed, as a society, in so far as that men are not forced into it by human compulsion. It is not voluntary, however, in the sense in which a club or a benevolent association is voluntary. I have not a right, as towards God, to remain out of His Church. He has thought at once of my interests, and of His glory when giving the Sabbath, the

---

* We refer to the discussion regarding the "kingdom," of which Premillennialists hold that Christ has not received it, or, if He has, it is only the kingdom of Providence (Dr. McNeile on the *Second Advent*), and will not receive it until His second coming. Against which it is argued, we think conclusively, that our Lord Jesus had a kingdom of grace from the beginning of human history, on the ground of what He should afterwards suffer as mediator; and that on His ascension He was formally (if we may apply such a word in this connection) installed, the work being now palpably done. Hence such language as that of John vii. 39. The gift of the Holy Ghost was the evidence to men of Christ's kingdom being rightfully set up. He was "glorified."

ministry, the Church, and the Scriptures, and I have no more right, as regards Him, to disregard His Church than to disregard the Ten Commandments. In just and violent reaction against that condition of things when the Church ruled as a great corporation, men's minds are in danger of forgetting this truth, and treating a divine, spiritual agency, of which the use is made imperative, as if it were a mutual-improvement society, to be entered or not, as one feels inclined.

The name of the Church in her present form is, and ever will be, Christian, not indeed by any formal enacting clause, but by natural causes overruled by the Lord. "And the disciples were called Christians first in Antioch." Some over-fastidious persons object to any names but what they find in Scripture; but they are not agreed as to one inclusive name. Some call themselves "disciples," some "Christians" (and some of them make the first syllable long for a distinct purpose), some "brethren" with prefixes of various kinds. They usually reflect on others for being called Baptists, Congregationalists, Presbyterians, or the like. They forget that these names are not in antithesis to Christian, but, seeing that there are peculiarities of administration, these names define and describe those who, being Christians, adopt them. The holders of these names are not always responsible for them; in many instances, as with "the people called Methodists," and the Quakers, they were given by unfriendly tongues. To object to the names is no more wise or candid than to quarrel with the naming of the streets, or the numbering of your houses. A man does not deny the unity of the race, who describes himself as an American, a German, or an Englishman. He would be thought crazy, if he refused to be known otherwise than as a human being, or an Adamite. So we can speak of Congregationalists and others without impugning the oneness of the Church of Jesus Christ.

Nor is this sufficiently obvious fact without bearing on our themes. Christian is the substantive: Episcopalian, or Methodist, or Moravian is the adjective. And this ought to be true of the ministry and the sermons. Their first, most obvious and pronounced quality ought to be that they are Christian. There are times, and there is a place, for sectional truth; but the staple of our ministry is to be Christian.

The Christian Church has officers. There were at

the beginning apostles. They appointed elders, ruling and teaching, who took the work from apostolic hands, and continued it according to instructions. So they carry it on to-day. They are successors of the apostles in so far as this that they do the same work and under the same authority, just as every patriotic American citizen upholding the fundamental institutions of this country is in succession to the signers of Independence. The "tactual succession" is an idol "graven by art and man's device," and has no place in the temple of God.

The great business of the apostles was to teach. Miracles attracted notice, attested the teachers as from God, and, having fulfilled their necessary uses, were withdrawn when the new dispensation had acquired its hold; as the wooden framework is withdrawn from beneath the arch when the mortar has set, as the wrappings are taken from the ingrafted branch where a vital union has taken place. Their great business they were to "commit to faithful men,"[*] able to teach others also.

The Christian Church has outward rites and sacraments of divine appointment. Two have a place of

---

[*] 2 Tim. ii. 2.

permanent value and authority—baptism and the Lord's supper. One symbolizes union, the other communion with God in Christ. In the one we are shown as ingrafted into Christ; in the other, as growing up into Him. Both are means of grace, and while no wise and intelligent Christian will disregard them, neither will he confound them with the source of grace, nor the agent by whom souls are renewed and sanctified. Probably in the violent reaction against the excessive sacramentalism of mediæval times, some Protestant churches have been inclined to undervalue these means. As they are adapted to our complex nature of body and spirit,* it is easy to err regarding them, either by excessive spiritualizing or excessive rationalizing. So, also, we may clothe

---

* It is remarkable that the hardest problems in psychology, and the most curious phenomena of life—on which a mischievous "spiritualism" has for thousands of years built itself—should have their place in that very union of the material and the spiritual to which the sacraments, with their complex character, have been adapted. One need not wonder that the same perverted ingenuity that made necromancers, conjurors, and every variety of oracle in heathendom, and found for them some plausible foundation in the facts of human nature, should have turned the sacraments into the coarsest kind of fetish, as has been done in Roman Catholic countries.

them with an awful and mysterious grandeur that repels the average Christian, as is done with the communion of the supper in the North of Scotland; or, worse still, we may degrade and vulgarize them, as was done when receiving the communion was made—as in Great Britain—a qualification for public office.

That ministers are charged with the administration of the sacraments does not rest on any supposed superiority in holiness, or even in knowledge. They are however, representative men in the nature of things, accepted by their brethren as teachers, constituted officers, and so far standing to the Christian society somewhat as the chairman, or the secretary, of a secular community stands to it; so that what the community in either case does, it does by him. Ministers are the organs of the Christian society, and the sacraments, having among other uses, this, that through them the adhesion of members is formally made and maintained, the official persons are charged with that which binds and represents the society. It is needless to add that all this is on the human side of the matter, the moral and spiritual efficacy of the sacraments depending not on "anything in them or in him that administers them, but on the blessing of

THE IDEA OF THE MINISTRY. 17

Christ and the working of His spirit in them that by faith receive them."*

These considerations regarding the nature of the Church, her officers, and sacraments, must determine in a good degree our views regarding the place and work of the ministry; and if they do, our labor is not lost in their statement.

To that part of our theme we now turn.

Our translators made no discrimination in the two Greek terms of the apostolic commission, for which they have given the one word "teach.†" But there is a real distinction. In v. 19, we have the Greek word $\mu\alpha\vartheta\eta\tau\epsilon\upsilon\sigma\alpha\tau\eta$, *make disciples*. When men believed and became disciples, the ordinance of baptism into the name of Father, Son, and Holy Ghost, gave opportunity to join the Christian society, and avow discipleship, and now they became pupils to be taught, and another word altogether is employed, $\delta\iota\delta\alpha\sigma\kappa\upsilon\tau\epsilon\varsigma$, teaching.

Here was a double work for the Church's officers, evangelizing and instructing the evangelized, or, in other words, the work of a missionary till men came under the sway of Christ, the work of a pastor after-

---
* Shorter Catechism. † Matt. 28. 19.

wards. Considering the variety of age, intelligence, and moral characteristics by which any of us must needs be surrounded, if we are to be good ministers of Jesus Christ we must be prepared for both these departments of apostolic work. While stationary, we must also be missionary. A man who only means to build up those who choose to come to him will usually have a contracting sphere of labor; while a man who neglects to feed the flock of God, in his eagerness to gather into the fold, will fail of one great function of the ministry, the perfecting of the saints.* The Lord makes us $\pi o\iota\mu\varepsilon\nu\alpha\varsigma$ $\kappa\alpha\iota$ $\delta\iota\delta\alpha\sigma\kappa\alpha\lambda o\upsilon\varsigma$, *pastors and teachers*.†

When we inquire what shall be taught, the Lord's words are sufficiently explicit. "Whatsoever I have commanded you." This does not exclude subsequent

---

* It has been proposed to read this well-known sentence (Eph. iv. 12) "for the perfecting of the saints for the work of the ministry," as if work were the purpose of their being perfected. This is, in fact, true in part. Saints do not go to heaven at their conversion, for this, among other reasons, that there is work for them to do. But while this reading would well suit the temper of an age when Christian *activity* has a fair share of attention, as compared with *spirituality*, it is not sustained by the construction. See Ellicott *in loc.*

† Eph. 4. 11.

direction by the Holy Ghost, but it takes away discretionary power from us, and shuts us up to our instructions. We are not plenipotentiaries, but "ambassadors" with defined and limited powers. We are not principals, but messengers, deputies, speaking with authority not inherent, but derived. Like the prophets who preceded Christ, we who come after Him must, instead of His divine and authoritative "Verily, verily I say unto you" (egotism inexplicable in one of such meekness, unless he meant to claim more than created dignity), ever say, "Thus saith the Lord." Looking around on a flock committed to us, we find some disciples by birth, and some disciples by belief, more or less strong and intelligent. What shall we teach them? All things whatsoever Christ commanded in person, or by His illumining Spirit; of whose teaching we have the record, we are bound to believe, in the later books of the New Testament.

This direction of our Lord rules out many themes that have found their way into the Christian pulpit. Science, for example, except as it may illustrate Scripture truth, is excluded. It is one thing to employ it as Chalmers did in his *Astronomical Discourses;* it is another to make the pulpit a scientific rostrum. This is no reflection on science, which has her own themes, pulpits, teachers, and appliances, and a noble ministry for man, and which always will be respectable and useful on her own ground, only making enemies among intelligent Christian men when she abandons it. *

This same idea may be presented in another form. A preacher is all the stronger for understanding the Greek grammar, and an occasional reference to it, when the elucidation of a passage calls for it, is natural and proper; but this is a very different thing from undertaking to teach Greek grammar in the pulpit. How good use a religious teacher may make of the

---

*In our own time an apparently serious breach appears between science and religion. We say appears; for it will be found that scientific men have given offense to religious, not as "scientists," but as philosophers. No man quarrels with the experiments, the observations, and the interrogations of nature pursued by "scientists." Their pursuits, aptitudes, or travels have given them special facilities. It is when they philosophize on the results they suppose they have reached, and assume that they have all the facts in their hand, that their special faculty is denied and the divergence from Christians has commonly begun. And when one talks of a conflict between science and religion, it is of the first consequence that he define his terms. What is "religion?" How much does "science" include? Did the magicians represent it in Moses' day?

facts of the world will be obvious to any one who has read such a charming book as *Bible Teachings in Nature;* * but discussions on natural history would not be to edification in the pulpit. A preacher of the gospel may range over all pastures; he may, like the bee, levy his tax on all that is sweet and attractive around him; but it is that the Church, which it is his business to feed, may have made good the promise of Isaiah concerning the holy child—" Butter and honey shall he eat, that he may know to refuse the evil and choose the good." †

The same limit excludes from the pulpit nearly all that comes under the general term of speculation. To guess; to " think out " ingenious surmises; to be undetermined and indeterminate; this is sometimes supposed to be the sign of great mental activity, and even force. Such a man is not " in ruts; " he is out of the beaten track, truly; he is " suggestive." But of what? A preacher of the gospel is not a builder, beginning at the ground and constructing a theology, or a theory of the universe. He is an embassador with instructions, a messenger with a message. Let

---

* By the Rev. Hugh McMillan, Glasgow. *McMillan & Co.*
† Isa. vii. 15.

him deliver his message. He has no business to say: "I have been thinking of this theme. I have reached such and such results with my present light. I give you my conclusions so far as I have gone; they may be different next week or month, as I get further light, and then—for I am perfectly honest—I shall report them to you with reasons." That is not, I humbly think, the tone for Christian preaching. It was proper enough in the Academic groves where Plato, Zeno, and Socrates gave their best thoughts to their disciples. But we are not, Gentlemen, heathen philosophers finding out things; we are expositors of a revelation that settles things. Our authority in speaking, like our right to speak, is founded on the word of the Lord. And it would, surely, be a little unreasonable to expect our fellow-men, as intelligent as ourselves, to repose with confidence on conceptions that are in obvious perpetual flux! That were to build on a moving bog; to anchor to a log, itself drifting; to set up landmarks of snow. They might well enough say to us, "Gentlemen, get something settled, and then come and tell it." We need not wonder if men cease to go to church on such conditions. We need not affect surprise at religious indifference, or the growth of all manner of abnormal mushroom crudities, springing up in the night which such speculation in the pulpit makes, and which must be treated with caution, since it is difficult to distinguish the edible from the poisonous fungus. Life is too brief; men's souls are too valuable; too little time can be had for spiritual affairs to waste any of it on such day-dreaming. When Jesus said, "I am the way, the truth, and the life; no man cometh unto the Father but by me," He spoke positive truth, which it is our business to echo. He indicates a road to the Father, on which no human engineering can make improvements. We are to set men's feet so far as we can on that road. Let authors, magazine writers, poets, and philosophers wander at their own sweet will gathering flowers and enjoying views over the prairie of unbounded imagination. We, my brethren, give ourselves to another task; we are to direct human pilgrims, according to settled and fixed commandments from the Lord, into the way that leads through the gate into the city.

One common result of the style of speculation in the pulpit now criticised is the recoil of the human mind into a credulous submission to authority, or what claims to be authority. I shall be very much surprised if there be not, in those portions of this country where positive teaching is lacking, a growth of those forms of the Christian faith, more or less un-Protestant, whose teachers claim to speak with authority not founded on an appeal to the commandments of Christ, but on a great indefinite corporation behind them arrogantly labeled the "Infallible Church."*

---

* It will be alleged, perhaps, that this Church-teaching is only another form of the authority we urge and which free thought repudiates. This is true in so far as all successful error has an infusion of truth in it. Romanism in its various forms is a skillful travesty of truth. But it substitutes the authority of a body of men—however ancient that body—for that of God. The authority of God's word is of another kind; and the appeal to it leaves the human mind free as to man, for it is in the hands of those who hear our appeal, and who can judge of our accuracy. The difference may be made apparent by an analogy. Imagine a lawyer telling a jury: "Gentlemen, my case is sustained by the universal body of jurists from the beginning: if the other side quotes cases to the contrary, they are not recognized by us as from the body of jurists. No one is in that venerable body but those who agree with us." His opponent says: "Gentlemen, my case is sustained by the statutes—here is the book. I shall read it to you. I shall hand you up the book, that you may examine it yourselves." This is the Protestant, Evangelical ground.

While it is said in Scripture "hear the church"*
on the small and practical details of the differences
among the Church's children, these perverters of the
right ways of the Lord apply the words to all the
principles that constitute the Christian faith. Their
Bible is only a private document of the Church. Our
Bible is the Church's charter, book of laws, directory and court of appeal. Their standard of time is
a very old and oft-repaired Italian watch; ours is the
unwearied sun.†

The same limit shuts out what may be called Ritualistic preaching. From long habit and church-usage,
a usage which once prevailed over this country, I
wear in the pulpit the gown and bands which are
known as Genevan, and were once worn by scholars

---

* Matt. xviii. 17: and that Church, by the way, in the nature of things, must have been in the first instance the congregation.

† It is of no use to say that if the Book is thus made everything, there is neither use nor place for a ministry. The answer is twofold. (*a*) The book calls for a ministry. He who gave it, and makes for it so extensive claims, does not regard it as superseding the ministry. He knows man's wants. And (*b*) practically the book no more sets aside the ministry than the admirable school-books of America set aside the great army of school-teachers who employ them. Men can do little more than copy God's methods.

as distinguished from others. They are convenient to me, and to all awkward and ungainly men, and as a pulpit uniform they save the people from the temptation to criticise our outer, when they should be improving their own inner, man. But I should not feel at liberty to preach about them, or to find occult symbolical meanings in them. What was proper enough when the Jews had a series of object-lessons and not a Bible, is a retrograde movement, a return to " weak and beggarly elements " in the Christian dispensation. This would hold, even if the symbolical teaching of the Ritualists were true in itself; but too often it is not. On the same principle, all that goes by the name of "Sacerdotalism" is excluded from our ministerial teaching. There is a true sense in which a minister, in common with all believers, is a priest to God,* but there is no true sense in which ministers are a distinct priesthood, and the special application of the word to them in Protestant literature is singularly infelicitous. The $\iota\varepsilon\rho\varepsilon\upsilon s$ of heathen and of Jewish language had a true place. He was a sacrificing priest. Our Lord Jesus Christ is such a priest.† But we seek in vain for any such designa-

---

* 1 Pet. ii. 9. † See Heb. v. 6; vii. 15, in Gr. Test.

tion in the Scripture for the Christian teacher. He is *Episcopos*, from his functions as overseer (Acts xx. 28); *Presbuteros*, from age or the qualities age is supposed to bring; and *Diaconos*, minister, from his being a servant; but never *Hiereus*.* And this is the more remarkable, considering what a gain it would apparently have been to clothe the ministers of the new religion with the honor and prestige of the established and recognized priesthood. But when this was done it was by a political and corrupt corporation, and not by the Holy Ghost.

While the positive rule that determines our themes is " all that I have commanded you," it is not to be understood that all the parts of the body of revelation are equally important. They have not all the *same* place. But they have all *some* place, and are essential in that place. "Thumbs and great toes" are not the body, but they are essential to archery and running; and Adoni-bezek's captives were no longer fit for war when they had lost them. A book on the

---

* "The Priests," says Archbishop Whately, "both· of the Jews and the Pagan nations, constantly bear, in the sacred writers, the title of *Hiereus*, which title they never apply to any of the Christian ministers ordained by the apostles."—*Origin of Romish Errors*, p. 95 (London edition).

rights of American citizens will not dwell at equal length on all the rights, nor at great length on those of a past generation; though it will often be needful to go back over the history of a law or an arrangement, in order to show its present bearing. This principle all lawyers understand, and it is not to be ignored by the expositors of Scripture. It is so, also, in medicine. There are cycles of disease, and new developments of suffering. We require men to grapple with the maladies of to-day; but to do so they must study the history of diseases, mode of development, conditions, remedies successfully exhibited in their treatment, that they may be competent to cure. It is so no less in the arduous labors of him who would labor for and under the Great Physician.

Once more, men's views of truth are affected by conditions of their minds, the training they have had, the circumstances around them, and "the times" in which they live. A wise and competent teacher will present Christ's commandments in obvious application to the wants of the hearers, so that their fitness shall be recognized, and that they shall have all the gracious effect of saving truth to them. For it is one of our comforts and elements of strength that true theology and true Christian life fit into each other. The Christian truth is not, as it is sometimes represented to be, esssentially different from all other forms of truth with which science can deal in the way of experiment; nor does it rest so exclusively, as is sometimes alleged, on positive external authority. When a man trembles at the thought of God and an invisible world, has he no experimental evidence of divine truth—no proof within himself that " it is a fearful thing to fall into the hands of the living God ?" When the Scripture declares that " out of the heart proceed evil thoughts, murders, adulteries," do we believe it only because it is there ? Do not we know within ourselves that it is true ? When the Lord talked with the woman of Samaria, was there nothing to impress but the probable credibility of the stranger ? Had she no evidence warranting her invitation, " Come, see a man that told me all things that ever I did; is not this the Christ ?"* And the same argument might be applied to conviction of sin, hope of pardon, peace of mind, fellowship with God, struggle with corruption, and victory over the world; all which come within the range of experience. When

---

* John iv. 29.

Elizabeth of Hungary, after rough treatment from an old crone, who should have been grateful to her, tells her story, she has experimental evidence of spiritual truth.

> " Let be—we must not think on 't.
> The scoff was true—I thank her—I thank God—
> This too I needed. I had built myself
> A Babel-tower, whose top should reach to heaven,
> Of poor men's praise and prayers, and subtle pride
> At mine own alms. 'Tis crumbled into dust!
> Oh ! I have leant upon an arm of flesh—
> And here's its strength ! I'll walk by faith—by faith !
> And rest my weary heart on Christ alone—
> On Him, the all-sufficient." *

We can rejoin to experimental philosophers when they invite us to the laboratory, as we point to human fears, sense of guilt, remorse, despair, or, on the other and brighter side, to hope, peace, reform, and life of holiness, " Come and see."

> " Oh, make but trial of His love,
> Experience will decide
> How blest are they, and only they,
> Who in His word confide."

To get, then, the mind of Christ, and to declare it,

---

* *The Saints' Tragedy* (Act III. Scene II.) by the late Canon Kingsley.

is the primary end of the teaching officers of the Church. The living body of sympathetic men, saturated with the truth and feeling of the book, must bring it into contact with other men, through that marvelous organ, the human voice, and with such aid as comes from the subtle sympathy that pervades assemblies of human beings. And while systematically teaching Christ's truth, as they have learned it by the Holy Ghost, they must never forget the power that moved them, nor fail to honor that Divine Person who not only gives, but has condescended to be, a "tongue of fire." This work of speaking the truth is the justification, the "reason to be," the honor, the dignity of the Christian ministry.

LECTURE II.

It was stated in the last lecture that the ministry is not to be regarded and studied by itself, but in its relation to the Church; and so the sermon is not to be provided for as a detached factor, but as one of a number of co-operating forces. The ball is for the cannon; and the cannon is for the artillery; and the artillery is for its appropriate place as a portion of the army. Whatever may be said hereafter of preaching in the Evangelistic method—where continuous teaching with the view of building up men is not contemplated—we here and now think of the preaching of pastors. We venture to think that—whatever may be done by extraordinary men, who attempt little beyond preaching, and who effect much by the influence so exercised over masses of men—to the average preacher the greatest amount of usefulness comes by his being a pastor. It is freely admitted that the apostles were not continuous laborers in limited spheres; but they were special agents for special work, with special gifts. It is freely admitted, also, that there have been apostolic men like Whitfield, John Wesley, and, in a different sphere, Nettleton, who accomplished the most noble results by preaching, apart from pastoral labor. But fully conceding all this, we adhere to the conviction that for you and me—ordinary men—it is the wisest thing to labor concurrently with our preaching in those other and related ways, which come under the general head of "pastoral work," over a limited field, and by persistence, continuity of effort, and force of known character, to supply in some degree the lack of special gifts and extraordinary powers. If ever there was any lack of *talking* faculty in America, we have the prospect of a remedy in a revival of attention thereto. "Speakers" enough we shall probably always have; but we want speakers who shall be pastors, and whose speaking shall be an integral part of an entire homogeneous pastoral work.

I propose to show the relation between preaching and the other parts of a minister's duties; and I place this topic here, because it will contribute something to our ideas as to preparation for preaching as a life-work, and also as to the making of the individual sermon.

A congregation is composed of a number of individuals, including many groups of families, with some general features in common, but with great personal diversities. Living in the same locality, and meeting frequently, particularly in their religious assemblies, the members exercise an amount of influence on one another, and any force set in motion among them has a fair opportunity to be propagated. What is the minister to the congregation? It does not matter, for our purpose, whether he is a member of it, or an outsider called to its help. We need not here raise the question whether he is one of a distinct order or not. This much is certain, he is not of a caste in any such sense as if the office were hereditary; or as if celibacy, or some other important peculiarity, marked him off from his fellow-citizens and fellow-Christians. And while a certain peculiar brotherhood must needs bind together, and ought to bind together, ministers, everything tending to make them a caste ought to be deprecated. For our purposes, it is sufficient that the congregation invites a Christian man of approved gifts and character to come and live among them at their cost, and labor for their own and their children's spiritual good. He accepts the position and the work, looking, indeed, over the heads of the people, and believing that through them his Master in heaven has beckoned him to this post of duty.

Now, to make the most of himself, what, on the ordinary principles of common sense, which the Scriptures never contradict, ought he to do? Obviously he *ought to know the people*. A medical man has many advantages from knowing the constitution of an old patient; but he may also judge of present and palpable symptoms, and give the best advice to one whom he never saw before. A lawyer may form a perfectly sound opinion on a case, of the parties in which he knows nothing but as they are in his brief or paper-book. But a minister's functions so essentially differ from the lawyer's and the doctor's, that acquaintance is desirable, and spiritual influences will commonly run in the channel of confidence and affection. How can he know them? New-Year calls and visits of ceremony are good as far as they go; but they do not go far enough. Men are " on their manners" at such times. Weddings and social meetings are a little better, for there men relax; but they have their drawbacks. People do not go to evening parties to meet their clergyman, and be "edified." They go to enjoy; and the average clergyman is rather afraid of the imputation of talking "shop," and rather ambitious of being seen as the generally well-informed man. I do not blame him for this: a clergyman ought not to be conspicuously behind any whom he meets as a courteous, intelligent, agreeable gentleman. He may not have time or inclination to go much into society; but it is as well that it should be known that he is a "pleasant man to meet," when he can afford it—neither a recluse, nor a boor, nor a Diogenes in his tub, ordering everybody "out of his sunshine."

To make the acquaintance of his people, a clergyman must go to their homes, see the family where the family lives, and converse with them in the freedom of their own homes. He may systematize this work; make it more or less formal;* prepare

---

* In some of the British churches ministers visit, once a year, along with an elder. There may be some advantages in this.

the people beforehand or not;* conduct devotional exercises in the family, uniformly or not; but he ought always to gain from going to the homes of the people. The generalities he delivers from the pulpit with easy confidence he should have opportunity to try on particular cases among his flock. His mode of life, training, conditions, habits of mind, differ from theirs in many cases. He ought to learn, and so come to allow for, their differences. And not

---

A wise deacon of spiritual and sympathetic character might be a great help in some instances. But, as a general rule, there will be more frankness with the minister "by himself." And a visit from the deacon *by himself* would probably effect more than if made as the attendant of the pastor.

* For many years I pursued, in common with many of my British brethren, the habit of mentioning from the pulpit the streets or localities in which visits would be made on particular days. This secured the presence of most of the family, and among plain people, a certain preparation. I see no objection to this plan anywhere. I wish we could have it, for the sake of thoroughness and as a check on desultory "calling." One of the best clergymen I ever knew, and one of the noblest of men, the late Dr. Urwick, Congregational minister in Dublin, had his congregation arranged alphabetically, and his announcements ran thus: "I hope to visit on Monday the families from G. to I." This plan entails some loss of time, as distinguished from the neighborhood method, as the "G's" might be widely scattered.

least, he should give himself a chance to form that "liking" for his people which is founded on knowing, and to make that subtle chain of interest which is only formed by contact. You see a mother in her nursery, holding her baby in her arms, looking into its pinched, pale features to find out, if she can, if the symptoms of life or of death predominate. Your heart enters into her anguish. You kneel down at your chair, and ask God, who gave her the mother's heart, to give her grace and strength; and you say what words you can of comfort and encouragement. Can you ever feel to her again, as to an ordinary member of the human family? And if the child is spared and grows up, is he not a little more to you than another child? A man tells you something of his life, his struggles, his sorrows, perhaps his sins; his lip quivers, and his eyes overflow in the recital. If you have the first elements of a minister's nature in you, you must feel and speak to that man evermore with some influential memory of the interview. Any ordinary minister who is to do spiritual good to his people must love them. But ordinary men found their affectionate interest on acquaintance. It is not love in general, and in the abstract, that makes a channel to the human spirit, but love to individuals, into whose faces, and in some degree into whose hearts, you have looked.

But a minister must go close up to his people, that they may know him. They will believe the more in his earnest desire to do them good, when they find him as a minister at their dwellings. They will hear him in a new spirit when he preaches. It is not quite true, that all the eloquence is in the audience; but much of it is there, as truly as the echo is in the bosom of the mountain in part, though in part also in the bugle-blast that evoked it.

The strangest ideas are entertained by some regarding ministers—ideas that nothing but contact will rectify. It is good for the people to see that he is human, " a man of like passions" with themselves, and as he goes among them a true, simple, natural, unaffected gentleman, walking on no stilts, free of all insolence of office, obviously fighting the battle of *his* life, as they are fighting theirs, they learn to believe that the sublime principles he enunciates from the pulpit are not for some retired, privileged spot inhabited by ministers, deacons, and their respective wives, but for common men and women who live, and toil, and enjoy, and suffer, and who must die and be judged.

But how does all this bear upon preaching? Much every way, as we shall see presently.

But "preaching from house to house," of the best manner of doing which, it is not needful to speak here, is only one of several ways in which to come near the people. They are capable of being distributed into classes. There are the very young, who are to be brought into, and kept in, the Sabbath-schools. Whoever else works there, the minister is to be in the van. It is common to say that parents cannot delegate their duties to a Sabbath-school teacher. Nor can ministers. We should be in our schools, know the teachers, encourage them, help them, give them, if they need it, a little salutary discouragement, and be known to, and know, their pupils. If one says, "I have not time," it is answer enough to rejoin, "For what are you there? Do not you know that these Sabbath-school children are your charge now, and will be your adult hearers in ten years?"

Above the grade of the children is another class— young men and women, many of whom should be, but are not, in the membership of the Church. A communicants' class* will reach them, and lead many, through the Divine blessing, to Christ, and to His table. A gentlemen's Bible reading, a ladies' Bible class, a workingmen's mutual improvement society, any suitable agency that brings minister and people together for a good object will do good directly and indirectly. One need not hold to the same form of effort continuously. Some things will get a fresh life under a new form or name. Only let these be conditions : that the pastor's eye is over all, and that as unobtrusively as he likes, but really he be felt for good in all; and that he come near his people.

Now, how does all this bear on preaching? In three ways at least, to be mentioned with but little illustration.

(a) The minister will be aided in selecting from the materials he finds in the word. He knows his people, their condition and wants. He is the observer of constant development of character. He

---

* This name is not familiar in America, but the idea may be realized under another name.

sees where the weak points are. There are matters of belief they do not understand. He will note them, and at a fitting time set them forth. There are practical duties falling into abeyance. Family altars are fallen, or the fire on them is burning feebly. He will magnify this priesthood and sacrifice of the home. The children are getting too much of their own way, too little of godly training. He will spend a few Sabbaths, perhaps, on the commandments. No one can be hurt when the fifth comes in its place. There are signs of loose morals in the community. The seventh or the tenth he will not slur over; in fact, it would be very strange if he did. And every pastor will find that a certain life is infused into sermons that have a fitness of this kind. There are certain lines of Bible truth over which we are carried in Seminary. Some of them, perhaps, were made deep and clear by a forcible professor. Over some of them, perhaps, we traveled often and painfully, in view of an examination. They have assumed an undue importance in our thoughts, and we are tempted to think that they must be of great interest to the rest of the human race. Yet, in point of fact, that portion of it for which we are responsible has no doubt about them, will not comprehend our argumentation, and feels no connection between it and daily life.

Not only will a man get the most valuable assistance where every minister has spent some, and many a great deal of, time—the selection of themes—but he will often get his best points and illustrations in intercourse with his people. Going among them, with ears open, eyes observant, and heart warm, he will see modes of life, hear forms of expression, witness human experiences, all new to him, familiar to them, the reproduction of which will bring him and his message near to them, and into their real life. For the sake of impression he means to describe a sick-bed or a death-bed. Many men go to what they read, or remembered, in books. Let him go back to what he saw among them. He would represent vice and sin; and he gives a catalogue of vices which they know little about, at least by his names. Let him call them as they do among themselves, and tell them the truth regarding them, as he does regarding Christ, the great sin-bearer, " in their own tongue wherein they were born." His preaching will have a new force and significance to them. It is undeniable that for want of this many otherwise most excellent men are ineffective all their lives. Their sermons are echoes, slightly modified in transmission, of the didactic or polemic themes of college and seminary life, or of the literature in which the subjects are kept under their continued notice. Their wheels are in rapid and regular motion, but they do not *bite*. They hardly know what is the matter. Neither do their people. Now and then, perhaps some one more shrewd than the rest asks: "*Cui bono!* All that being so, what is it to me? What, in fact, do we care about it?"

(*b*) By this means a thoughtful and observant man is aided in adapting his methods of preaching to his people. Take an average theologian, of bookish habits and scholarly tastes, and an average workingman, and what a great gulf is fixed between them. How embarrassing a long conversation would often be to both of them! It would be a miracle if, on merely general principles, and without knowing him, the theologian could hit on the language that would be clear, and the aspects of truth that would be suitable to him. The minister must bridge over that gulf. Is it not one of the reasons that account for the mass of men that do not go to church, that they have no feeling that the talking will be on the plane of their lives? Is it not the fact that for a long time Methodism made its triumphant and blessed progress through the ministrations of comparatively illiterate men? Is it not the fact that in many instances the memory of their success is still so strong as to create some prejudice against a learned ministry? What is the remedy for those who are educated, and who cannot go back, if they would, to an illiterate condition? Why, to go among our people, learn their ways, modes of thought, habits of looking at things, and so acquire the power to speak to them, and not over their heads.

You think this involves a world of trouble! Well, Gentlemen, it is for that we are made ministers. If we are not willing to take trouble for souls, let us leave our places for braver men, and go into politics, or law, or trade, or anything that will give us substantial results without pains—if there be such a sphere. What do we require of our missionaries to India? Why, that they learn, with pains and trouble, the language and the idioms of the people, so as to be able to speak to them. They are useless till that is done. And are not souls in Connecticut, New Hampshire, and New York, to be approached in much the same way as in Gujerat or Lodiana?

(c) But there is yet another gain, greater, perhaps, than either of these—namely, *power of impression*. A man will often pay a visit, where he feels little immediate good is to be done, but he says to himself, "It will bring them under the Gospel next Lord's day; or it will secure their hearing it without prejudice, and with a kindly disposition towards the messenger." They expect him. They will be vexed if he does not call. Shall he stay away because their ideas are inadequate? or shall he go, like the Master; "lest we should offend them?" Persistent, patient effort in a man's home makes the preaching a very different thing to him in the pulpit. "He believes every word of it—he told it over to me many a time in my own house, only not so grandly as he is telling it now." Gentlemen, when we wind up our organ on Friday and Saturday, and grind out its tunes on Sabbath to the people, such is fallen human nature

that a good many think we are just going through
our professional round, and that when it is done it
is "done with," as far as we are concerned. But
if we come to a man on Monday and press the
same truth on him, just as earnestly as we
did on the congregation on Sabbath, he begins
to think there is something in it. One of
the most successful clergymen I ever knew was
a good preacher, but would never have been
distinguished merely as a preacher. Two years
ago a gentleman of intelligence and influence told
me this suggestive story of him. "I was sent to
school in Belfast," said he, " and my father brought
and introduced me to the Doctor,* and provided a
sitting for me;" (a good example, by the way, for
all parents in the like circumstances.) "I attended
very well for a couple of months, till I got a little
knowledge of the town, and then I thought one Sunday I would go and hear some one else. So I did.

---

* I allude to the late Rev. Dr. Morgan, of Belfast, Ireland, of whom an instructive biography has appeared, under the editorship of his son—also a faithful minister. No man known to me made more effective use of all the gifts he possessed "in the work of the ministry."

Next morning, as I was on my road to school, I met the Doctor, on his way to my lodgings. 'William,' said he, 'I missed you from church yesterday, and I came round to see about you.' That fact," said he, " that he missed *me*, and came to look after me, fixed my attendance, perhaps saved me." Gentlemen, we are to reverse that maxim of the law, *De minimis lex non curat*. Nothing is too small for our notice, if it helps our ministry. I have the pleasure of numbering among my friends a minister, of whose usefulness it is impossible to speak in too high terms, and whose ways of working I know, because when at college I had opportunity to observe them.[*] He is the type, to my mind, of the class of ministers required to evangelize our lapsed masses in the great cities. He had a plain, small, and inexpensive church-building, adapted to the people. No man

---

[*] The Rev. William Johnston, the late efficient Moderator of the Irish General Assembly, is still an active and vigorous minister, whose unselfish and most patient labor in the cause of orphans—among many other public services—have resulted in a system, through which every child of the Church, in clerical or lay family, when deprived of parents and means, is provided with education, home, and Christian care, at the cost of the Church—a noble work surely in a country like Ireland.

could find a pretense for staying away in the incongruity between his own shabby appearance and the handsome surroundings in the church-edifice. Many of his people were workingmen, who were then paid their wages on Saturday night—a bad plan, now abandoned in many places in the interest of the tempted. My friend knew how great was the danger to a man who had spent six long days in a mill, or a tenement room converted into a workshop, released on a Saturday night, with his week's wages in his pocket. His sermons were ready before Saturday evening; and about the time when a man might be supposed to feel the attractions of the "public-house," he sallied forth for a round among such of his parishioners as he knew to be "weak." Rapidly passing from house to house, with the question, "Is Thomas in?" "Has William come home?" "Where is George?" he bestowed warning, commendation, counsel, as the case required, and in fact did everything short of seeing his endangered sheep to their beds, before he sought his own, often at late midnight. Now, this seems very prosaic work—it has few æsthetic attractions for a cultivated man. But Thomas, William, and George felt it "in their bones" as they went to church next day, and heard their pastor preach. And their wives—why, "Mr. Johnston" was their guardian angel! For remember, the preserving of Thomas is not only help to his wife, it is care of the children, is the saving of a family, is the hiding of a multitude of sins, and the saving of a soul—perhaps many souls—from death.* The congregation which enjoyed such labors is now large; William, Thomas, and George have become comfortable, if not wealthy. They paid their few shillings for their pews, when they were poor. They paid more shillings as they rose; and well they might, for how much the Church helped their elevation; and their children are now men and women, and bringing their young ones to hear the good man who baptized and married their parents.

This is a form of acquired power which we are in danger of losing through our short pastorates. Do we sufficiently consider the difference between the brilliant performance of a man who comes from one knows not where, to go one knows not whither, and the sermon that has behind it twenty years of unself-

---

* James v. 20.

ish, faithful friendship to the hearers? Something will be said, later, regarding the connection between our current methods of preaching and short pastorates; but, in the meantime, I crave leave to emphasize the point that "patient continuance in well-doing" gives a minister's sermons a force that is *sui generis;* "there is," as David said of Goliath's sword, "none like that, give it me." Let your fathers tell you of the patriarchs of the pulpit, whom they used to hear and see; for to see them—severe as was their dignity—was a sermon. Times have changed, indeed; but there is no reason in the nature of things why this element of power might not be secured and conserved to a far greater degree than at present, if we and our congregations were only wise in our generation. Why, on our present plan, a boy or girl has hardly had time to know the name and look of the pastor till he is saying farewell; and has hardly learnt to discriminate between his successor and the miscellaneous crowd of men who were "on trials," till that successor is also delivering his "Valedictory." All which, let us hope, a wiser and more spiritual community will ultimately change.

There is one wrong impression which might possibly be caught from the drift of these remarks, namely, that personal contact with the people, and diligence in the good offices of the ministry, is to become a substitute for ability, freshness, and force in the pulpit. I do not mean that: I should greatly deprecate such an idea. These forms of personal contact with the people are urged, not to supplement weak, common-place, "milk-and-water" talking (the milk often left out), but to accompany, illustrate, and enforce vigorous, instructive preaching, and to co-operate harmoniously with it in forming character and winning souls. When Arnold preached to his boys at Rugby, he was listened to all the more because he knew his Greek, and would stand no nonsense on Monday; and his manly uprightness and thoroughness in school made his sermons in chapel all the more effective. So there is interaction between the visiting and the preaching. The visit of a preacher is all the more valued because the preaching is good; and the preaching is all the more appreciated, because the visit was paid. When men and women, with high and yet constantly repressed aspirations, quit dry-goods, groceries, and housekeeping details, and go to church to hear a sermon, which they are sure will be to them like a summer breeze, or a morning of mountain air, not only from what they have heard before, but from what they know of the man, his personality mingles itself with every sentence he utters; and when he makes a visit at their dwelling, he brings into their home-life something of the largeness, nobleness, heavenliness, which they link in their memory with his sermons. Such, at least, is my ideal; how far it is from being realized, all men know. But, poor and feeble as we are, we should be still poorer, if we did not hold up before us the conception of a genuine, consecrated ministry, including all the life of a man who has received, like Timothy, the *Charisma*, "the gift," and who gives himself "wholly to these things." *

In conclusion, let it be said that all this argument is based on the assumption that the minister is a thorough and good man. If he be only veneered,

---

* How forcible are these words written to Timothy (1 Tim. iv. 15): ταῦτα μελέτα, εν τούτοις ἴσθι, "let these things be thy care, be in these things." What things? The reading of the Scriptures to the people, the exhortation (sermon), and the doctrine, or teaching (lecture, or expository preaching), v. 13. See Ellicott on the passage.

or varnished, or gilt; if he is one thing in the pulpit, and another out of it; if his sermons are no part of his life, but only oranges stuck on a pine tree; if he is a mere official person giving so much pleasant sound for so much money and position; if he is only an artist, selling his wares; then the less he comes among the people the better. He may wisely act on the plan, *Procul este! profani*. But if he be solid wood throughout (and it is the solid and hard wood that takes a polish), then the nearer the people come to him the better for moral and spiritual influence. And the experience of the Church is that the pastor effects the most in the end who comes into closest personal contact with his charge. No amount of organizing, no skill in creating machinery and manipulating "committees" is a substitute for this. Who feels the power of a tear in the eye of a committee? The minister who would be like the Master, must go and, like Him, lay the warm, kindly hand on the leper, the diseased, the wretched. He must touch the blind eyes with something from himself. The tears must be in his own eyes over the dead who are to be raised to spiritual life. Jesus is our great examplar.

"Standing where I stand, and weeping where I weep, he enters by the openings which grief has made into my heart, and gently makes it all his own. As my brother, he insinuates himself into me through the emotion of our common nature, that so I may be borne up with him into the regions of spiritual light and liberty. He takes hold of me by my sorrow, that I may get hold of him for deliverance from my sin." * "It is enough for the disciple that he be as his master." † "Let this mind be in you which was also in Christ Jesus." ‡

---

* Arnot's "Roots and Fruits of the Christian Life."
† Matt. x. 25.
‡ Phil. ii. 5.

LECTURE III.

In the imperfect and divided condition of the Church of Christ, her faithful ministers have many temptations to turn from their main theme, and not a few difficulties in the way of prosecuting their purely spiritual work.

The Church, for example, is parted into sections, and the division has not always been made or maintained in enlightened love. A man is tempted to be sectional in his preaching, to dwell on what has relative, controversial, or denominational importance, so as to distort the proportions of the body of truth.* It will thus come to pass that the greater, admitted, undisputed, common truths receive cursory treatment, while strength and time are laid out in emphazising those which seem to constitute the

---

* Our fathers used to speak of a " body of divinity." Whether they saw it or not, there is something very suggestive in the phrase. Every member in my body has not an equal impor-

"reason to be" of one's particular branch. And it is not perhaps unreasonable to assume that the smaller the denomination, and the smaller the apparent reasons for its distinct organization, the greater will be this temptation. An intelligent and candid man, insulated by a few beliefs from those to whom he otherwise belongs, can hardly help feeling as if called on by implication for a defense of his separation. So the essential truths, by which the souls of men live, may be pushed out of their commanding position, and a generation may grow up to whose Christian life they become too little necessary. Denominational truth has its necessary place. Great discretion is needed to confine it strictly thereto.

Vehement controversies have the same tendency. Just as in the siege of a city an accident may render an insignificant tower the key of the position, for the sake of which, for the time, the rest is comparatively forgotten, so a doctrine from being controverted may

---

tance; every one is useful for some purpose in its own place, and it would be mischievous to take any one from its place and apply it to another purpose than that for which it was formed and intended. So every truth of God has its place, and we are to keep it there, and give it its relative prominence.

have given it disproportionate attention, and may continue to receive it long after the real conflict is over; for the echoes of great pulpits, like those of a trumpet among the mountains, are frequent and far-resounding. Meantime the positive, uncontroverted truths are let alone; and a truth forgotten is of little more value to any one than a truth disbelieved. We shall not be able to dispense, for a long time to come, with conflict of thought, especially where men may be expected to feel most deeply; and in this, indeed, is the valid defense of our symbols, creeds, and confessions. It would be delightful to live in the open air, and on the broad savannas of general truth, if we were only let alone. But sophists and "philosophers," and "scientists" and crotchety men, "even of our own selves," arise and attack us, and we are obliged to throw up defenses against them, in the shape of articles, and doctrinal positions, so as to keep our ground, and transmit our heritage to our children. As they shift the attack, we have to set up barriers; hence our symbols are often bulky, and men do not want to take them down lest it invite the enemy again. And the misfortune is that the Church is blamed for encasing herself in a line of fortifications by the very "unreasonable men" whose action made the bulwarks necessary and numerous. While this necessity remains, the most we can do is to guard against the dangers. The truth which we set out in battle-array against a foe may not be the bread with which to feed the children of God. "Without are dogs" that keep up a continual barking, and we have to assure the timid flock within of safety; but we must not, while silencing the noise, forget to feed the sheep with food "convenient for them."

Those early and heroic preachers who built up the primitive Church did not escape these distracting annoyances, and they did not shrink from inevitable conflict; but neither did they allow themselves to be diverted from the work of positive truth-telling. When they mention Jesus Christ, they can say of Him, "Whom we preach, warning every man, and teaching every man, that we may present every man perfect in the day of Christ." Col. i. 28. This avowal of the Apostle Paul ought to be engraven on every preacher's memory, and burned into his conscience. It is Jesus "Whom we (solemnly) preach" ($\varkappa\alpha\tau\alpha\gamma\gamma\varepsilon\lambda o\mu\varepsilon\nu$) for the message is momentous in the highest degree; belief of it is life, rejection of it is death. "Warning" (νουθετουντες—putting it to the νους) "every man, and teaching every man." The two words cover the ground. Men are sinful. Nor is this an evil chance that has happened to them. They are to be blamed for it, and to be shown their sin. And they are to be taught, to be shown the way of forgiveness and life, that they may walk in it. The two words well correspond to the actual case of the earliest apostolic preaching. "Repent and be baptized (as believers), every one of you, in the name of Jesus Christ, for the remission of sins." (Acts ii. 38); or "Repent ye, therefore, and be converted, that your sins may be blotted out." Acts iii. 19. Men need to be shown their sin; hence, "warning every man:" they need to be shown the Saviour; hence "teaching every man."

Nor is there any latitude allowed, as if some could dispense with the warning. "Every man" needs it, for every man is a sinner; and if it be true that too many lay down their Christian profession with fatal facility, may it not be because they took it up without any duly pungent sense of sin and ill-desert? They had no such conviction as left a permanent impress on their minds of the essential evil and hatefulness of sin. In a natural reaction from that style of teaching that made such and such exercises, and so much conviction a *sine qua non* to admission to the Church, is there not danger of overlooking that reasoning of righteousness, temperance, and judgment to come, in which Paul engaged? We cannot, indeed, too eagerly or too frequently cry, "Come to Jesus." But to make this call intelligent and emphatic, we must needs assign Scriptural reasons. We must not scruple to say, "Come! for you have sinned. You are guilty. If you do not, you will die; for the wages of sin is death." This carries the step of "professing religion" out of the region of mere sentiment; it rests it on conviction. We utter an invitation to One who is indeed "altogether lovely;" but we give it, and without disguise, to all who are altogether unlovely, and whom we are to help to this self-knowledge.

"I really felt," said one of no common acuteness, "that when I joined the Church, I had done a most gracious thing, and laid the Church under great obligations to me, so eagerly had I been entreated to take this step." They who "join"* in this temper are likely enough to require "humoring," indulgence, and attentions innumerable. Have they not obliged the minister, elders, and deacons, by consenting to "join?" Obliged men by taking deliverance from guilt and hell at the hand of a compassionate Redeemer, who bought the deliverance with His life! Let us not be afraid to put the facts as they are; let us be true to the truth of things. We are not "of the schools," this or that. We are teachers of Bible-truth. Let us be pre-Raphaelite, showing men sin, guilt, danger, loss, ruin, as they are. We may draw fewer on this plan than others seem to do; but our net will not so often break. The quantity is less important here than the quality. The stream of Christian profession may seem narrower on this plan, but it will be deeper. Church-members will know where they stand, will have positive convic-

---

* Is it not possible to get a better phrase than this for advancing in the enjoyment of Christian privilege? for surely the word misleads, at least in the case of multitudes who were born into the Church, had their rights owned in baptism, and who grew up under the Church's teaching? A young man does not "join" the land of his birth the first time he registers or casts his vote.

tions, and instead of requiring perpetual incense from the Church, as from a community they have patronized, they will rather feel like the returned prodigal: "I am no more worthy to be called thy son; make me as one of thy hired servants." And when the ring, and robe, and shoes, and kiss, and feast, are given them—such gifts as no slave could receive and be a slave—they will know that they are not of debt, but of grace.

Nor is this double work included in preaching Christ a thing "done and done with" so soon as men have "received the atonement." It is to be continuous. Till the ear of the saint is closed in death, this sound is to fall upon it. It is not one law that condemns a sinner, and another that guides a saint. Nor does a believer cease to have to do with the law, or with the sin it reveals or condemns. He is pardoned, adopted, saved; but he is a sinner till "death is swallowed up in victory." "Sinner" is the substantive for him, qualify it as you will by foregoing words. "That we may present"* (not as a sacrifice, but as a piece of work to be approved)

---

* Col. 1. 28.

every man "perfect" (τέλειον, see Matt. v. 48) "in Christ." Maturity of Christian life is thus acquired by "every man." The law which was written on the heart, and obeyed in the earthly life of Jesus, is written also on the heart of the saint. He delights to do God's will. This is the aim of a true minister. Like Epaphras, he will be always "laboring fervently" (αγωνιζομενος) in prayers, that his charge may stand perfect and complete in all the will of God." (Col. iv. 12.) So says the noble and unselfish Paul, "To which end I also labor striving" (again αγωνιζομενος) "according to his working who worketh in me mightily. (Ch. i. 29.)

Here, then, Gentlemen, is the commanding theme of your preaching. Around the sun of this central Christ-doctrine, all other truths revolve as planets or as satellites. Why did He come? God pitied sinners. Why must He die? "Without shedding of blood there is no remission." Why do we need Him? We are dead in sin, under the law's curse. What are we to do with our sin? Carry it to the cross. How can it be removed? "The blood of Jesus Christ cleanseth from all sin." What shall men believe? That Christ is able and willing to save. To whom shall they go? To God in Christ. In whom shall they trust? A personal, living Jesus who was dead, and dieth no more. How shall they loathe their sin? By looking at the crucified Christ. How shall they vanquish it? In the strength of the risen Jesus. Ah! but the way is long and hard, and the struggle is unutterably wearying! Even so. There is no help for it "but to run with patience the race set before us, looking to Jesus." Men need to be awakened. The Crucified One is the most awakening sight in the universe. There is no attraction like that of the cross, if men are to be won. Nothing will melt a sinner, if his heart is to be softened, like a pierced Saviour (Zech. xii. 10); nothing to give life, if a dead soul is to be quickened, but the touch of the living Saviour; nothing to sustain, if a living soul is to be fed, but the living bread; none to carry through, if men are to conquer, but He who hath loved us. "Culture" is one of the cant phrases of our time. Gentlemen, as preachers we are to promote Christian culture, by bringing the dead branches to the living Vine, that, grafted into it, without priest or sacrament, or a rag of human righteousness between, the life in Him may enter them; and by keeping them, as far as teaching and example can do it, abiding in Him, that they may bring forth fruit. You would be "edifying" preachers? What does the figure in the word suggest? Why, you set men on the foundation and you build them up on Him. You would be useful preachers? Then, remember, in the day when the fire shall try every man's work of what sort it is, the eloquence, the tact, the poetry, the philosophy, the curious felicity of words, the manifold gifts and graces that were not directed to keeping before men Christ as Saviour, Lord, Master, Lawgiver, Example—not a priest only, to snatch us from pain and miserable ruin, but a King to rule us and recover us to God, "a priest *upon his throne*"—will be among the wood, hay, and stubble. Ah! many of us, one fears, who are applauded now, will be poor then in comparison with obscure and lowly preachers who preached Christ, and whose work will shine resplendent, as gold and precious stones, in the light of the great White Throne!

"But," says some one, "I shall be precluded from a large portion of Scripture by this rule." Far from it. Look at the fine, fanciful, spiritualizing of the historical books to be found in a large class of writers, whose school dates from Origen. Do not their very exaggerations prove the reality of Christ in them all? Look at the epistle to the Hebrews, full of Christ! But who understands it, if ignorant of the Pentateuch? The dreary records of apostasy, humiliation, partial penitence, and recovery of the Jews, seem far enough from this great theme. But they only seem so. What is their lesson to us? "Neither let us tempt Christ, as some of them also tempted him." 1 Cor. x. 9. The Psalms are often meditative, experimental, sometimes imprecatory of stern wrath on the Psalmist's wicked foes, because external prosperity was then the sign of divine favor, and when the sacred writer calls for their humiliation and ruin, he asks that God would declare, in the only language then understood—that he would prove by the only test then recognized—His displeasure against them. But have we no Messianic Psalms? It is true the prophets often seem obscure, abrupt, and unintelligible, mainly because we have given them too little study. Isaiah was not hopelessly such to Dr. Addison Alexander, nor is Daniel to Dr. Pusey: and they spake of Him. "To him gave all the prophets witness."

And this suggests the wisdom of taking to a larger extent than we do, chapters, or parts of chapters, and expounding them. We set out bits of Scripture in great beauty, like the separate tiles of a mosaic floor. Let us be expository to a greater extent, and the people will have the opportunity to see the pattern. We are liable to distort separate texts, and to misplace their messages. Let us help the people to look at groups of truths as they are set side by side by the Holy Ghost. "When my own mind is not very full," said a useful preacher, "I like to get hold of a large piece of Scripture." Not that an honest and effective expositor will find or make this work easier than textual or topical preaching; for it requires thorough study and honest effort to bring words written to Jews, or Christians eighteen hundred years ago, into the plane of our life. But it can be done; and when done well, an intelligent and devout hearer will be apt to feel that he has been addressed by the Lord, more directly than in many sermons equally true and effective.

That some definite idea may be conveyed on this subject, let a few sentences be here devoted to its consideration.

Expository preaching does not mean a rambling paraphrase of a chapter or a portion of a chapter, with a dexterous turn given, now and then, to the inspired words, so that they shall hit current events. Nor does it mean a devout meditation, such as one finds in the practical notes of Thomas Scott's "Commentary"—admirable as they are. Nor does it mean a subtle, ingenious twisting of the facts or minor incidents of Scripture, so that they shall all be made to disclose vital, spiritual truth. The illustrations of this style of Bible-use are abundant in the mystics, and in various types of modern teachers, of undoubted good intentions, but whose "readings" suggest to ordinary men that the divine word is elastic, capable of sustaining anything an ingenious fancy suggests. They are continually reading between the lines. Nor is true exposition perfectly illustrated in saintly Matthew Henry, or a class of works modeled on the plan of his, where various interpretations of the same Scripture are given with devout reflections founded on each—"if it be the true interpretation." A certain feeling of insecurity attends an intelligent hearer, under this instruction. " The fire-brands and the foxes employed by Samson, according to some authorities, mean "—so and so. "If this be correct, then we may learn" such and such lessons. "Or, according to others, they represent" so and so. "If this is the correct rendering, then we may learn" such and such lessons. Lessons taught in this loose fashion are felt to be hypothetical, like their basis. The "if" of their premises runs on into their conclusions. Nor, finally, is the expository preaching, to which we give hearty commendation, a general godly talking concerning a particular chapter, when almost any other would have served equally well, which begins nowhere in particular, which is interspersed with feeble appeals— "my brethren, is this your happy case?" and of which one feels, when it is over, that there was no particular reason why it should have stopped there more than anywhere else. Such "expounding" has brought into disrepute the true "reasoning out of the Scriptures,"* for which we plead, just as loose, inconsecutive, feeble preaching—"extempore," perhaps, in the literal sense—has brought discredit on the method in the pulpit, which men almost universally employ at the bar, on the platform, and in the

---
* Acts xvii. 2.

Senate—a discredit so deep that it is said that ministers preaching without notes have sometimes placed paper before them, and affected to use it, thus by a "pious fraud" saving the people from the indifference they would have felt if they had supposed their pastor merely talking to them out of a clear head and a full heart.

By expository preaching we mean that in which a minister, having, by the aid of grammar, dictionary, and all proper helps, learned for himself what meaning the Holy Ghost intended to convey in the passage he has in hand, and then what uses we ought, in harmony with the rest of divine teaching, to make of it, and having filled his own understanding, and warmed his own heart with this truth, tells it to his people, with clearness, simplicity, force, and fervor. They are supposed to have their Bibles in hand, to examine his references where they are adduced as proofs. The selection should be so made that the parts of the passage shall have a certain unity and concentration of purpose. One deep impression should be made. Now, it may be alleged that this is effected in substance in a sermon: and happily many sermonizers do fall into an expository method.

But we are more sure, it must be admitted, of making the impression the Lord intended, when we give the truth in the exact settings in which inspiration has placed it. Let me illustrate. A minister wishes to preach on the sin of robbing God in the matter of property. He can get a text in Malachi,* of great force and pungency. Scriptural illustrations abound, and he may preach a very useful, and often quite needful, sermon. Or the same preacher may take eleven verses of the Acts of the Apostles,† and give an exposition of the miracle of judgment in the opening of the Christian dispensation, corresponding to that by which God warned the Jews in the matter of Achan, as they entered on their promised land. He sets forth the temper, condition, generosity of the converts; shows how a spirit of liberality was in the air; how soon credit came to be thought of in the Church; how two persons conspired—a degree of guilt greater than individual sin—for a man will often do what only a more hardened transgressor can talk of; how the iniquity was exposed; the darkness of the crime and punishment all the more apparent standing out in relief against the grace being enjoyed

---

* Mal. iii. 8.   † Acts v. 1–11.

and the mercy being displayed. What is the gain of this method? Why, the memory is charged with facts, instead of abstract principles. A large portion of God's word is presented; and so the Holy Ghost, I humbly think, is honored. A vivid idea is given of the condition of the primitive church, and of the authority with which the risen Lord clothed his saints. All the impression is, moreover, made that could be expected from a disquisition on robbing God. And finally, if the expositor has done his work faithfully and effectively, whenever his hearers afterwards read that section of the apostolic history, it will be luminous before memory, understanding, and imagination.*

There are some considerations in favor of consecutive exposition, as of Epistles or sacred biographies. Thoughtful hearers will be interested.

---

* Miracles, Parables, Psalms, no less than incidents and arguments, admit of effective treatment in this way. The well-known volumes of the present Archbishop of Dublin (including his exposition of the "Epistles to the Seven Churches") are scholarly, honest, sober-minded, and generally safe, while they show what good use may be made of classical and patristic literature in ascertaining or in illustrating the mind of the spirit. In entirely different styles Leighton (on Peter) and Candlish (on 1 Cor. xv.) are masters.

They are not indeed the majority in most congregations; but they are the most worthy of consideration. They are the belts that convey and redirect power. There is a generation that does not relish this consecutive teaching, that misses the joy of guessing what is to be talked of. The younger persons who frequent city churches, particularly in the evenings, and whose deepest feelings are not interested in the service, do not like what assumes on their part memory, which they do not exercise, attention which they divide with many other matters, and attendance which is with them a matter of chance. But one is hardly to turn away from a useful method of edifying the Church, because the "casuals" do not value it. We are here more concerned about the manna for the host of Israel, than the taste of the camp-followers.* There are many incidental ad-

---

* The lectures on the Epistle to the Romans, by Chalmers, offer a splendid example in one style. The "Life of David" has been frequently used for expository purposes, nowhere more effectively surely than in the recent volume of Dr. Wm. M. Taylor, the vividness, discrimination, and devoutness of whose lectures entitle them to the careful examination of students, and should commend them to the attention of general readers. In an entirely different style may be mentioned "The Royal

vantages attendant on the expository method. Two only we shall mention.

(*a*) When the fire of Christian feeling is burning low on the altar of our hearts, far more than by any vivid pictures of divine things, or fervid exhortation, will it be kindled and fed by contact with the very word of God, set forth in its native force, and allowed to speak for itself. This has been the experience of the best minds.

(*b*) The power of producing able, ornate, finished sermons in the essay form is to most men limited. They must needs go back on their store. Suppose Bacon, Fuller, Macaulay, Lamb, or even John Foster, to have been under obligation to give an essay twice or thrice a week, along with all other duties such as ministers must do, and this for years, how soon a change of parish would be desirable! But we venture to think there is no such limit to the power of instructing, edifying, and deeply interesting a congregation for many years, on the method of making, say

---

Preacher," a series of lectures, not continuous, on Ecclesiastes. Their method, however, should only be followed by men assured of their possession of such poetic faculty and scriptural anchorage as Dr. James Hamilton enjoyed.

one-half the addresses expository. For a minister doing this duty conscientiously acquires a fullness of mind from his Bible which facilitates sermonizing and every other department of his work. Nor is he so liable on this plan to get into a rut of thinking and teaching as on the ordinary plan of preparing sermons.

The principle that positive truth regarding Christ is to be the staple of our teaching, excludes, I humbly think, much foreign matter that finds its way into the pulpit. I do not refer to social, or æsthetic, or purely political matters. Touching this last, it is right to say that in days gone by the ministers of this land were the instructors and leaders of the public in civil affairs. This is sometimes forgotten now by noisy and interested demagogues who object to ministerial expression of political views opposed to theirs: but the ministers of America inspired with their lofty thoughts, and prayed into success, the Revolutionary struggle. Crises may come when fidelity to Christ demands political teaching from ministers. But these are extraordinary. We speak of ordinary conditions of life. Our observation applies to a different class of discussions.

There are, and always have been men everywhere, trying their strength upon Christianity. We are under no obligation to turn aside to notice every assailant, and endeavor to set his argument in its proper position, so as to be able, in the intelligent judgment of our hearers, to upset it. There are many men undertaking to deal with Darwinism, or with the views of Tyndall and Huxley, in their pulpits, who seem to me to be wasting their power. Think, Gentlemen, for a moment of the most intelligent congregations to which we ordinarily preach; how many men are there in them who could intelligently state the philosophical views and scientific opinions of such men as Professor Tyndall? Are there twenty, or fifteen, or ten, or five? In many cases none. It seems to me a waste of energy to be compelled, first of all, to set up a fortification in the name of some man, explain to the congregation what you are hammering at, and then proceed to overthrow it. As a general thing, we may allow those things to take care of themselves in their own plane. We do the best we can when we set forth the truth in the way in which God presents it to us. I do not wish to be understood in making this statement, as decrying or depreciating in the least the most valuable and eminent labors of men who, as professors in colleges, as editors and writers, deal with these inquirers and objections. They are in their proper place; we owe a debt of gratitude to them; and we need not fear to leave the matter in their hands. They will deal with it, and effectively. If I, a minister, were to preach on political matters, it is not likely I could get a hearing from the editors and politicians. They know, or suppose themselves to know, much more about these things than I do; and have I any right to suppose that I shall be able to edify college professors and learned men by dabbling, in the pulpit, with their abstruse scientific questions? Why, they know these topics much better than I can pretend to do : and if they are wise, they would be glad of a little rest from them on the Lord's Day. Let them have it. Have I any reason to suppose that I shall be able to present the attractions of the theater in the pulpit, on the Lord's Day, in such a manner as will satisfy the ordinary theater-goers of the city? Every night they can have them in far more fascinating fashion than I can offer. Just as little reason have I to suppose that I shall attract scientific unbelievers by scientific expositions from the pulpit. But there are certain questions everlastingly asked by the human soul—deep, grave questions—which it is for us to answer, not as of our research or inquiry, not on our authority, but ministerially, as messengers delivering a message, as embassadors bringing terms from the Lord God Almighty. We have to make known Jesus Christ; we have to declare a revealed way of life, and to win assent to it on the divine authority. We need, that we worthily make this presentation, meekness and grace, manly courage and fidelity. A short time ago it was my lot to pass a few days in the extreme north of the State of Michigan. While I was there, I met my countryman, the Governor-General of Canada, who made a visit to the place. At the fort of Sault Ste. Marie, a salute of seventeen guns was fired in honor of His Excellency—guns never to be pointed, let us hope, towards Canada in any other way. All were delighted with the Governor. We were all thorough Americans, with a due appreciation of our national advantages, and their immense superiority to monarchical institutions. The grace, the ease, the intelligence, the affability, and the courtesy exhibited among us produced a deep feeling of admiration and respect for the representative of the British Government. There at least nothing was thought of but the good side of royalty and nobility, and nothing spoken of but the satisfaction of mutual friendship. But, Gentlemen, if we would but think of it, we bear the Commission of a King, our Saviour, far above all worldly dignities, and we plead for Him and represent Him to men. With what love and devotion ought His presence to inspire us! and with what courage, dignity, and confidence we should speak in His name to men! Oh that we may have given us so to labor that His holy cause suffer no harm at our hands!

LECTURE IV.

So far, Gentlemen, the argument running through these observations has been of this kind: The Church being as we have represented it, what should its ministry be? Again, the aim and design of the ministry being as we have represented them, by what means should its work be prosecuted, and what place does the sermon occupy to related and auxiliary agencies? And if we have ascertained generally the plan of preaching, what, in view of the Church's nature, and the purposes of the ministry, ought to be the themes of the pulpit, and what their proper treatment?

We have now before us, in a general way, the work of a preacher, or, more exactly, of a pastor; and before coming to the processes of making and delivering a sermon, the previous question may be fitly put and discussed in this hour—what preparation can we make for the work of preaching?

Physical considerations are not despicable, as many a feeble-bodied preacher knows. You cannot determine the strength of your chests, or the vigor of your constitutions; but you can conserve what you have received, by proper food, little enough of it, pure air, and sufficient exercise. Charles Simeon, I remember, told his young men that the first requisite of true hard reading was that they should take good care of the third mile-stone out of Cambridge, walking out every day, going round it, and making sure that no one had carried it away. No one can prescribe just what another ought to do. I had much good advice given me gratuitously when I was doing the full work of a teacher, and the full work of a student, when the only reply I could have made must have been, *Necessitas non habet legem*. But, so far as it is possible, let nature alone, and reserve your physical energies for the time when you will be expected to be always at home to receive callers, and always abroad among your people, and at the same time to produce sermons, addresses, speeches, lectures, and "remarks," not to say articles, as birds do their songs.

A minister ought to be a well-educated man, in

those branches of human learning that are not professional, or rather, that are common to all the professions. The reasons are obvious. A man may be spiritual and theologically well-instructed, whose orthography varies from the popular standard, whose grammar is uncertain, and whose reading in profane history goes little farther back than the Declaration of Independence. But the mass of mankind will doubt the capacity of a teacher in religious things, who is conspicuously deficient in common education. Have you noticed that our Lord, lowly as was His home in Nazareth, is never criticised for lack of such propriety, but, on the contrary, that his knowledge of " letters " * excited the amazement of his hearers? The prejudices against God's message are already so many that we ought to do nothing to justify or increase them, to omit nothing that we can do for their conquest. Even the writing of a good hand is not a despicable accomplishment, Gentlemen, for many will form an estimate of your taste, culture, and education, from your letter, before they have an opportunity to learn the solid qualities of your heads and hearts.

---
* John vii. 15.

It does not at all follow because a minister does not parade learning in the pulpit that he is without occasion to use it. The mass of the people have a good education within reach, and many avail themselves of the opportunity. All the questions of the day are discussed in the popular magazines, newspapers, and serials. Multitudes get that little, dangerous knowledge which enables them to ask questions. None are held back by veneration. Reverence for institutions or for traditions does not restrain our young people from bold inquiry. We must be so far abreast of the current of general thought and literature as to be able to answer intelligently, and with discrimination. There is an intercourse with capable and intelligent men to which we are called, and from which we should never shrink—it is an opportunity for usefulness—in Boards, Committees, and the great work of education, and in which all the acquirements we have can be utilized. A minister conspicuously deficient in intelligence, however devoted he may be, would soon lose his legitimate influence. He would be spoken of as a good creature, or as they say in Scotland—" a good body." It is always a loss to the cause of religion to create the impression that it only gets hold of the weaklings. It is always a gain, where it is seen that a man can be at once strong in common sense, vigorous in mind, well-informed, a king among men, fitted to rule by force of mind and weight of character, and at the same time habitually bowing in lowliness before the cross of the Lord Jesus. God forbid that ever the Protestant clergy should come to be what the priests of Romanism and of the Greek Church in too many instances have become, in mental training, and capacity for affairs, "the lowest of the people." We are for teaching and preaching. It is to be remembered that a quotation from the Bible will not always be an answer. It will sometimes be a *petitio principii*. You will be told there are previous questions: how do we know yours to be the meaning, and how do we know it to be a revelation?

It is commonly believed that for the purposes of composition, mastery of our English tongue, and cultivation of taste, a knowledge of the Greek and Latin classics is essential, the word "classics" being commonly limited to the Pagan writers. In this free atmosphere it may be permitted me to say—without being roasted as a literary heretic—that we have possibly overrated this department of education, and that the suggestions that come to boys in the reading of Ovid, Lucian, Horace, and Sophocles, do more evil than is commonly thought*—evil enough to counterbalance the intellectual gain. But there are other classics than the heathen; and it would be an omen of good if candidates for the ministry at least took Eusebius, Tertullian, and John Chrysostom, and others of a noble band, to whom we

---

* The writer does not allude mainly to impure associations, but to the mythological suggestions. How natural to a reflecting boy—possibly not an adept in the evidences of Christianity—to say to himself, "As sincerely as we believe in our religion, these cultivated men believed in this legendary dreaming. So coming races may look back on our superstition." It is no answer to say that sooner or later he must know this fact. Here he does more than know it. His mind is held down to it for the most impressible years of his life, and the years in which reason and conscience are needed for restraint and guidance. The writer declares what he knows when saying that mischief is often done here. Intelligent Bible-teaching ought to be given concurrently with more than common earnestness.

of the reformed free churches have given none too much attention.*

There have been able and most successful ministers with "small Latin and less Greek;" but that is no reason for ministers missing the knowledge—when it is accessible—that would enable them readily to consult the Hebrew and Greek originals, understand the point of a critical exegesis, and appreciate Winer's New Testament Grammar, or Trench's Synonyms. We say readily: one hears the Hebrew Bible read by theological students with a slow deliberateness that is not all born of reverence for the sacred text, and which suggests that (as we soon cease to do what we do with difficulty) the after references to the book will not be frequent or enthusiastic. Men who have only skimmed the school-books, or been squeezed through, ought not to

---

* The experiment now in progress in Lafayette College, at the cost of Mr. Benjamin Douglass, with the enlightened co-operation of Professors March, Owen, and Ballard, is not only full of interest, but full of hope, on other grounds than those indicated in the text. We have nothing to lose by the raising of the question, *Whose are the Fathers?* (See an admirable volume with this title—London: Longmans, Green & Co.—by the Rev. John Harrison, in review of the claims of the Anglo-Catholics.)

count their present condition a finality. To carry on one's own reading will be a valuable means of culture, an agreeable change of work, and will secure a permanent mental possession.

For, remember, that the great business of your life is to be the exegesis of the holy Word. You may not call it by that name to the people: call it opening up the Scriptures, reasoning out of them, anything you will, only provided you have the thing. To know, with the aid of grammar, dictionary, collation, and examination of the argument, what the Spirit of God intended to convey in a passage, is a first requisite to honest, faithful, and effective preaching. With all your gettings, get the capacity to do that. It is even more important to see it, and know it, and be able to state it, than to vindicate it and show that it is just as it ought to be. The truth is, there is a way of rationalizing the Gospel, without being the least *Germanized*, which does not help, but hinder. We enunciate a truth as reported in the Word, and proceed in a strain which, reduced to plain statement, would run thus: "Now, brethren, the Lord says the wages of sin is death, and the gift of God is eternal life. I shall now proceed to show you good and sufficient reasons why He should say so," and we proceed with our argument. The solemn assertions on the Lord's authority, if the people understood them, *were proof*. But we proceed with our argumentation, which may possibly be less cogent, or less clear, or less interesting than is desirable. The weakness or obscurity of our demonstration comes to be connected in the memory of the hearers with the propositions involved; and if they are received finally, it is not because the Lord has said so, but because we have established His right to say them.

Gentlemen, we are heralds, rather than logicians. We announce the Lord's will; many truths of the Word we may fearlessly declare without waiting to argue. They will do their work. Some of them instantly connect themselves with convictions or demands in the human soul, and fit them as the key fits the lock. Some of them can afford to await proof. Some of them get their proof as other Scriptures are explained, as the stones hold one another in the arch. But to be able to echo the triumphant and authoritative utterances of God's word, we must know them. Here is " ample scope and verge enough" for our energies. How many books have been written on Genesis? Is it exhausted yet? Why, the last work on it, by Dr. Lange, with the additions of Dr. Taylor Lewis, is far the best. But is the book exhausted? On the contrary, it never enlisted the study of so many as at this moment. For how many volumes have the Psalms furnished a basis? Is the mine worked out? Who is to penetrate the prophecies of Ezekiel, Daniel, Jeremiah, and the rest of the prophets, continents which enthusiastic devotion has yet only surveyed, with less accuracy than the Livingstones and Bakers have attained in Central Africa. Yet generations of saints will yet feed in these desolate and waste places, as they now seem to many. Therefore, with all possible urgency and solicitude we beg you, as candidates for the ministry, get yourselves ready for the exegetical study of the holy oracles. Elementary Biblical criticism is too often a dull study. I remember when the Hebrew Professor, who had been helping our slow and stumbling feet through Daniel, announced to the class that "our next hour introduced us to the Chaldee," my nearest neighbor drew a long breath,

UNJUST ESTIMATES. 91

and said, "I did my honest best with the Hebrew:*
now I give up!" There must be no giving up
here: a year's despondent inactivity here means comparative feebleness for a life-time.

It is the fashion to decry theology in our time.
The opponents of that noble science mean no harm.
They only do not understand. What they cannot bear
is metaphysical or speculative hair-splitting, on the one
hand, or on the other sharp-cut, clear statement and
defense of truths they do not like. Let a man put
his theology into attractive forms, and they will
tolerate it; or let their own views be urged forcibly
by a trained dialectician, and they make no objection.
We can no more have exact religious thinking without theology, than exact mensuration or astronomy
without mathematics, or exact iron-making without
chemistry. The puddlers at Pittsburgh would probably think a technical disquisition on the methods of

---

* The writer notes with pleasure that the class-book in Great
Britain was then Elias Riggs' Manual of the Chaldee Language, with an introduction by Moses Stuart, of Andover, whose
services to the cause of Bible Exegesis are as heartily appreciated in Great Britain as here. The volumes were imported
from New York—an early installment of much literary property
now moving eastward.

desulphurizing iron ore a tedious business; but some one must master the chemistry of iron and steel making, or it will not go forward. Let there come along an earnest, plain-spoken, clear-brained man, who can put the technical chemistry into their own tongue, and illustrate it by effective experiment before their eyes, and he will interest any body of iron workmen in America. A plain man told Dr. Dabney that the reason John Randolph was so appreciated by the common people was, "Because Mr. Randolph was so instructive; he taught the people so much which they had not known before." * So it will always be. Men object to what they do not understand or do not like in theology. Be you diligent, patient students of it, that you may put its exact truth in intelligible forms, and teach the people knowledge. †

While theology, as a whole, ought to be studied with care and thoroughness, there are portions of the "Body of Divinity" that deserve special attention, because there is at the present time more than usual reference to them. While deprecating, in a former

---

* *Sacred Rhetoric*, by Robert L. Dabney, D.D., a valuable work, to which we shall have occasion again to refer.

† Ecc. xii. 9.

lecture, the pulpit refutation of scientific imputations formally or informally cast on the Bible, it was not intended that an educated ministry should disregard them. It was only meant that formal and specific treatment in the pulpit is not usually to edification. But for the peace of his own mind, for the maintenance of perfect confidence in his own cause, and for the purpose of satisfying individual inquirers, a minister should be thoroughly conversant with the evidences of Christianity. It is one thing for a medical man to have mastered chemistry and pathology; it is another for him to pour out his knowledge of the same on every patient, and to spend his time in demonstrating the impudent falsehood of every pretender to "miraculous cures," whose circulars are sent to his patients.* It is one thing for a lawyer to be well-informed in the principles and rules of law; it is another altogether to marshal his erudition for every conviction in petty larceny. So while we do not recommend the employment of

---

* Any one who takes the trouble to inquire, will be amazed to find from the booksellers to what a large extent the "scientists" owe a market for their books to the clergy, who laudably and naturally desire to see what can be said against the truth.

pulpit-time in the overthrow of every caviller, we do urge the importance of mastering the evidences of Christianity.

There is some need, also, for more attention to the Romish controversy than has hitherto been given. It includes the question of questions in Europe at this moment. But it is only a small and relatively unimportant part of the argument that is now enlisting alike divines and statesmen. Long before this inquiry into the contradictory obligations of Roman Catholics in Protestant countries arose, there has been, and long after it has lost its interest, there will be, the deeper, wider, and farther-reaching question of salvation by grace, or salvation by something else. Americans have been indifferent to these issues from strong confidence in their institutions, and from a certain contempt for Romanism, natural enough in the circumstances. This continent has not yet had a strong and capable expositor of Romish views. The system has been poorly represented, timid, and rather asking toleration than influence. But it has passed out of that stage. It is capable of adapting itself to all governments and all conditions of society. It can use the resources of the poor; it can, like the priests of Baal, in Ahab's time, feed at the table of the State. That we need not pay much attention to it because it will never dominate this Republic is an egregious mistake. A long way on this side of ruling it may obstruct, retard, and injure. Poising itself between two great parties in the State, and unfettered by any but its religious pledges, it can exact and secure concessions in its own interests, and to the damage of the Republic.

To regard it as contemptible as a system of argument and religious belief, is an insult to the human understanding. That fabric on which for more than a millennium the mind of Europe was occupied, strengthening what was weak, defending what was exposed, and making it strong, compact, and imposing, is not a disorderly pile of loose stones and rotten timbers. As a system, it is concatenated, logical, and, if you admit a few of its fundamental principles, its conclusions are irresistible. If I put the statement strongly it is because I feel earnestly on the subject, when saying that many admirable Protestant ministers would find themselves embarrassed in discussion with a well-educated member of the "Society of Jesus." It is thought, indeed, illiberal to have strong convictions on a topic of this nature; but it is one thing to afford the fullest rights to every citizen, and the amplest consideration to his conscientious convictions: it is another to be blind to the tenets and tendencies of a system which is, and cannot help being, a political corporation hardly less than a religion, and which has already enough of organization and force to make it the interest of politicians in our great centers to secure its patronage.*

This topic may be studied in the department of Theology, or in that of Church History—to which, if I may judge from my own recollections, a young minister will find himself under great obligations. Much, of course, depends on the grouping of themes and the special aptitudes of both teachers and learners. In my own case, I studied Theology under a professor who was not exact, or profound, but who

---

* It is not only in the action of Romanism on the public schools that there is cause for anxiety. In many parts of the country, under most mistaken ideas, Protestant parents intrust their children, particularly daughters, to Roman Catholic educators. The education is second-rate, but it is showy; and the influence is almost uniformly un-Protestant.

had many of the elements of a great and noble man, and who managed to give the impression that all truth was revealed for adequate and appropriate purposes, that it was godlike to love it, to live it out, and to employ it for the enlightenment of the race, and that it was unspeakably mean to feel that we had nothing more to do about it, after we had secured for our individual selves a hope of rest and peace. On the other hand, in the department of church history, it seems to me, there was shown to me the difference in principles at the points where they strike human conscience, and affect human interests, and there was laid in the mind the solid conviction that in the final issue even here, life, for the man, or the institution, is indissolubly linked with " submission to the father of spirits." *

You may perhaps be surprised when I urge as another element in preparation for the work of preaching a thorough acquaintance with the English

---

*Heb. xii. 9. It affords me pleasure to mention that the able Professor, here alluded to, the Rev. Dr. Killen, of Belfast, Ireland, is still rendering effective service both in his chair, and by such works as *The Ancient Church, The Church of the First Three Centuries*, etc.

Bible. Though it is under revision, the changes in it will not materially affect its phraseology; and though we have often to advert to the original for exact shades of meaning, to the mass of our hearers the English Bible is, and deserves to be, the standard of appeal. To be familiar with it so as to quote it from memory, with point and accuracy, is of no trifling importance. Even in point of language and style, it represents one of the best periods of English literature. It is often singularly grand in its simplicity, and singularly terse and emphatic in its nervous Saxon. A verse rightly put and rightly repeated, will often fix a truth better than a whole sermon. I once heard M. Merle D'Aubigné deliver a long, elaborate, and very able discourse, at the opening of a Theological Seminary in Great Britain. I do not remember a single idea in it all except one, which he stated and enforced with the question from the Epistle to the Hebrews: "We have had fathers of our flesh which corrected us and we gave them reverence: shall we not much rather be in subjection to the father of spirits and live?" How often a man will tell the minister he heard him preach so many years ago, ingenuously adding, "I do not remember the sermon, but I can tell you the text." How often a solemn and awful truth can be uttered in the impressive phraseology of the Scripture, which it would seem harsh or arrogant to put in our own— "The wicked is driven away in his wickedness;" "It is a fearful thing to fall into the hands of the living God;" "How shall we escape if we neglect so great salvation?" "They shall utterly perish in their own corruption." How frequently a sin is indicated in a phrase which all men understand, which if we try to render in our roundabout conventionalisms, we dilute the meaning, perhaps mislead altogether. How often the tenderest pathos is brought to bear without the least pomp of words, or elaborate painting: "As a father pitieth his children;" "As one whom his mother comforteth;"

Turn ye, turn ye, why will ye die?" How much rest and strength one comes to associate with its report of benedictions in Psalms and sermons, of speeches and arguments, through which is breathed the tone of calm and confident assurance: "Blessed are the pure in heart: for they shall see God;" "I know whom I have believed;" "Beloved, now are we the sons of God." "There remaineth, therefore, a rest for the people of God." Gentlemen, if you would speak to the conscience and heart of your fellow-men, if you would subsidize all their old memories, and enlist all their sacred associations on the side of your cause and your Master, have thorough and easy possession of your English Bible.

"And how, one asks, is this to be gained?" Some have been at pains to memorize it. There is a more excellent way. Read it for your own devotional purposes so much, enter into the spirit of it so deeply, that you shall have it literally "by heart." Men of taste, in thorough appreciation of Horace, Cicero, Shakespeare, Tennyson, Longfellow, can quote them accurately and at length. But what are these great masters to any man, in comparison with that which the Bible is to us as Ministers of Jesus Christ?

I would almost venture to put among the elements of preparation for preaching some little experience in teaching. A superficial person is apt to suppose that to tell a thing once is sufficient for all purposes. A thoughtful person knows the contrary, knows that in the common affairs of life we often repeat and reiterate the instructions we wish to be remembered and acted upon. So a thoughtful teacher soon finds; and one of the main objects of the preacher is to teach. The teacher varies his phraseology, puts his points variously, asks questions, illustrates, suggests, employs shifts and expedients to insinuate definite ideas into the mind. A brilliant and successful advocate once told me that it was idle to suppose that one simple didactic statement would reach the understanding of the men on a jury. "I never assume anything of the sort," said he; "I go over the same ground again and again, not always in appearance, varying the language and mode of presenting the idea, until no more can be said about it." And we must remember that twelve jurymen, on oath to decide justly, may be supposed to have their faculties on a tenser strain, and their intelligence higher than the average of an ordinary mixed congregation. Men find this out practically in teaching; and so not only because a minister is all the better for having some practical knowledge of teaching— for Sabbath-school and other purposes—but because teaching is so essential an element in good preaching, a little experience in practical instruction is to a candidate for the ministry a substantial advantage.

Nor would I omit from the list of elements of preparation some endurance of the *res angusta domi:* a little personal conflict with straitened circumstances. It is a good thing to have learned the value of money: to have acquired the power of sympathy with those who have it not:

"*Non ignara mali, miseris succurrere disco:*"

to be independent of luxuries: to enjoy looking at the store-windows of Broadway and think how much is there that you can do without: to be poor, and yet not tempted to mean and sordid devices: and to be able to preserve self-respect when money is a rapidly-diminishing quantity. Gentlemen, I need not hide from you that ministers, as a rule, are not rich. They are not so much below other professions, place for place, as is sometimes alleged; but they have fewer remedies than their ill-paid fellow-laborers in law or medicine. Yet, they are often obliged to study well the buying power of dollars: and they are none the worse for it as men and as ministers. The men in the ministry who are rich by inheritance, or by felicitous arrangements, need special grace to keep them " up to pitch " in effort. They are specially liable to sore throat, weak bronchial tubes, delicate chests, and nervous affections, that require rest, travel, and variety of scene. The difficulties of narrow means have not ".repressed the noble rage" of all ministers. One of the ablest writers yet produced by the Baptist or any other denomination, the Rev. Dr. Carson, lived in a thatched farm-house, and often wrote, I am assured by one who had means of knowing, at the kitchen fire, rocking his child's cradle with his foot. Many young ministers are poor men, but that is no reason, Gentlemen, why you should be poor ministers. " A. man's life consisteth not in the abundance of the things he possesseth." His bodily life does not—his intellectual does not—his moral does not—his ministerial does not—his spiritual life does not. He may be " poor, yet possessing all things."

Only one thing more I feel constrained to specify in this Lecture, without at all claiming to have included all the elements of preparation, namely, habits of personal devotion. Lately I saw the statement in one of the religious newspapers, that a minister was kept so long writing sermons that he had no time to study his Bible! No man studies well, here, who does not pray well, any more than in Luther's time.*

When I was passing through my preparatory classes, I had the advantage of association with a group of eleven or twelve young men, who met once a week for the private study of the Bible and prayer. It was in our own rooms. We were friends, in perfect mutual confidence, not afraid of one another, and yet our intercourse was purified, and elevated by our common pursuit and our united prayers. I was one of the youngest and the least able to make a contribution to the

---

* The following extract is from a very thoughtful article in the *Interior* of Jan. 7, on " the Bible in Church."

" What prevents our ministers from adopting, more generally than they do, the practice of expository preaching? It is the most profitable, they will all say. They would much prefer it. What is in the way? The people look for a ' regular sermon.' Are we, then, under ' bondage' after all? A minister in an important charge once told us that his time was so taken up in writing sermons that he actually had no time to study the Word of God. That was a strong statement, but we can readily believe that if a minister had the idea that two elaborately prepared ' discourses' were expected from him every week, he would subordinate everything to the attainment of that end."

common stock ; but I think I could truly say, that no one set of lectures did so much as these weekly meetings to prepare me for being a pastor. The intellectual quickening was the least element in the preparation. I got an idea of the truest of all fellowship—fellowship in Christ. I learnt how love to the Master and love to saints go hand in hand, each strengthening the other. I learnt that a man does good to his people when he has come to count them a circle of his friends, and spontaneously—not officially—to carry them on his heart.

When we parted, each to go on his way, we agreed on a time—the hour of our meeting—for remembering one another, and exchanged lists of names and addresses. I have my copy still. Of the eleven, two are in heaven. The other nine are vigorous evangelical ministers. It is twenty-six years since we parted. I do not doubt they remember me, and I still keep that "sacred tryst."

LECTURE V.

PREPARING A SERMON.

It may seem to you, Gentlemen, as if we had lingered unduly among preliminary considerations, and approached with needless delays the immediate matter of sermonizing. If so, please set it down to the tendency in the lecturer's mind to desire not only clearness in a subject, but clearness all the way up to it. Possibly, if you recall these thoughts after some years, your judgment will justify the slow movement; for you will have seen that in the end principles determine particulars, and that men will pray, and preach, and labor generally according to their conceptions of the church's business, and of their own place as ministers.

The priestly theory, for example, marks the Roman, the Greek, and most heathen systems. It shapes the labors of the clergy in almost every particular. They can only "officiate" with the prescribed robes: they can only move on the line of rubrics: they succeed in the degree in which they are accepted as official representatives. To get a bit of brass in the form of a cross hung round the neck next the skin, and out of all men's sight; to "christen" a baby even without the knowledge or approval of parents; to anoint a man even though he is incapable of responding to any movement secular or spiritual; to give "Christian burial"—whatever that exactly means—to the dead, who in life would have given nothing good to the celebrant—these are admissible in such clerical life. Preaching is a subordinate duty to preparing for, or administering sacraments.

Take the churches as a whole, and classify them, and you will find that as the priestly idea, or the High church idea, goes up, the sermon goes down. In Roman Catholic countries there is little preaching except in Lent, and then it is not as a rule by the pastors, but by itinerant friars, whose function is preaching. In some instances their preaching is good of its kind—in some remarkably adapted to popular effect. But, as a rule, it does not admit of, nor receive too close inspection. The preacher in a cathedral, for example, is raised in a high pulpit;

the audience is not seated; there are no preliminary devotional exercises connected with the sermon; the preacher enters the pulpit, crosses himself, and commences, "In the name of the Father, the Son, and the Holy Ghost," proceeding directly with his discourse, the most effective portions of which are usually sensuous pictures of our Lord's sufferings, emphasized frequently by reference to a cross, or crucifix in or near the pulpit.* I have seen such a preacher exhibit, in tone and gesture, all the indications of the most vehement feeling, and yet with certain peculiarities of face which led me to retire, so as not to annoy anybody, and look at him with an opera-glass, and to my amazement and disgust, his

---

* There is a strong tendency in the Roman Catholic system to isolate the crucifixion, and so represent it as to appeal to the mere sensuous feeling. The genius of Protestantism, in closer harmony with the Bible, leads to ample exhibition of the dignity of the Saviour's Person, and to connect that, not so much with mere physical pain, and pathetic recital of touching details, as with the fact that he became "obedient to death" in such a form as identified Him with the promised seed of the woman, and the substitute of sinners. Romanism has a high place for the crucifix, and the "Son of Mary." Protestantism knows nothing "save Jesus Christ, and Him crucified," (1 Cor. 2-2)—Jesus Christ, the glorious Person, giving value and power to the work, "Him crucified."

countenance did not betray the least feeling. He was at a safe elevation, performing his rhetorical pantomime in a purely mechanical way, and yet not without its effect on a very illiterate audience. There is not only more good preaching in Connecticut than in a whole Roman Catholic country like Spain or Portugal, but there is not in one of these so much preaching, good or bad, as in one of our States. Protestantism has produced, by its proximity and rivalry, more preaching for Roman Catholics in America than they would otherwise obtain.

Let me now indicate some of the points to be assured in the making of a sermon; the immediate details every man must fill in according to his own aptitudes, and the habits of mind he has been led to form.

1. Be sure you understand the subject you undertake to present, so far as you bring it to the attention of the people. We do not mean that you know all about it, for there are many themes by their very nature bounded by the limits of religious thought, as the Divine nature and attributes, the future of the soul, the constitution of the Person of the Messiah, and the operation of the Holy Ghost in regenerat-

ing. What we mean, is, that so far as your theme is to be set forth, you should have clear, definite ideas of your own, not half-thoughts, but thoughts, not dim and nebulous images looming through haze and mist, but distinct conceptions that admit of being put into intelligible language. It would be awkward, if some one had the right to interrupt a preacher in a flowing paragraph of graceful verbiage, with the demand, "Pray, tell us what you mean," if he could not tell. A good test of your own grasp of the subject is found in talking it over with some one, if below your own intellectual plane, all the better. If you cannot explain it, and vary your phraseology, and put it colloquially, it is not likely to be of much value in the pulpit. You may imagine you have ideas, when you have only words. You may deem yourself a master of language, when it is language that is the master, and you the slave. If, captivated perhaps by one brilliant suggestion, perhaps by the very sound of the words in a text, perhaps by one striking application of a passage, you have been tempted to begin a sermon on it, and find you do not have clear, consecutive thought about it, lay it aside, until you can read, study, examine, and master so much of it as a sermon holds. The first requisite to teaching is knowing.

2. Be sure your theme is one the people can understand. There is much with which your professional education has familiarized you that is out of their depth. They have no ground in common with you in certain directions. There are controversies metaphysical, theological, even experimental, into which they have never been conducted, where your argumentations would be to them as algebraic symbols to one who never learned mathematics. You are writing in cipher and they have not the key. They make a little effort to understand, fail, sit down in despondency, with a little vexation and irritation of mind, where you ought to be regarded by them with complacency; so they not only lose their time, but they are ill-disposed to you next time you preach, and have so far formed a habit of inattention.

It is not meant that at the beginning of your sermon the people understand the subject as well as you do. If they did, there would be little need to preach. It is meant that your arguments, appeals, explanations are such as they can be made to understand.

The consciousness that they are taking in your ideas, and being carried from ground over which they had been before, and on which you and they stood in common at the beginning, into entirely new ground, is eminently pleasing, and is frequently expressed by " interesting."

Nor is it meant that the people should be able to reproduce your arguments and conclusions. Often this would be impossible. But your sermon is not, therefore, useless. There are many things to be proved, of one of which an intelligent hearer would say, " I could not give the steps myself, but I know it can be proved. I heard our pastor on it, and I know he satisfied me." Or an objection is to be disposed of, and a candid man might say, " I know it can be met, for I heard it discussed, and it was made clear to me, though I cannot recall the answer ; but I know there is one."

Let a gentleman on the hustings discuss political issues in a strain of unintelligible abstractions, and he would never be asked for a second speech. Let a lawyer address a village jury in language and with considerations fit only for the pages of Coke upon Littleton, and he would have few cases. And let ministers preach, however ably or elegantly, above the comprehension of the people, and their general and kindly verdict will be that "they would be admirable professors, but —" The plan of Ezra and his friends is indispensable to success.* "So they read in the book in the law of God distinctly, and gave the sense, and caused them to understand the reading."†

3. Be sure your theme is great enough for a sermon. Remember many of the people will have only one or two such in the week. A thing may be true,

---

* In connection with the reading of God's Word, something needs to be said. There is, in some quarters, a growing idea that the reading is to be done, but whether intelligibly or not is of little moment. This is offensive to good taste and good sense, and is vicious in principle. It puts the reading of Scripture among the mere *preliminaries*, to be got through with, as if the reader said : This is secondary—a mere form ; presently the real thing comes ; *I* shall be heard. How can a man truly magnify God's Word in his sermon, if he has belittled it in his reading ten minutes before ? It was my misfortune to hear the Scriptures read in the Protestant Episcopal Church in Rome, so rapidly, monotonously, and unintelligibly, that the Pope himself could not have complained of it as giving the Bible to the laity in the vulgar tongue. It was clearly an *opus operatum* performance. It had to be done *pro forma*. Its value lay not in its reaching the mind, but in its being gone through.

† Neh. viii. 8.

Scriptural, intelligible by you and the people, but not of such moment as to entitle it to be the burden of a sermon. That thorns were a part of the curse on the earth, and that our Lord was crowned therewith, when made a curse for us; that a rainbow was a covenant sign to Noah, and that a rainbow was round the throne in the apocalyptic vision; that the napkin and linen clothes lay in order in the empty tomb, showing that our Lord did not steal out of it in unattended and nervous precipitancy, but left it as a man leaves his house where he is free; that Jesus spoke to the young girl he raised up, with paternal tenderness, *Talitha cumi*, as we should say, "Darling, arise;" that Matthew calls himself "the publican," and that the other Evangelists omit the offensive word; these, and many things like them, are interesting in their place. They are "bits of scenery" such as artists pick up, but not large enough to make a picture. They are fine as illustrations and allusions, but they are not great enough for sermon themes. Take the great outstanding facts, the Alps and Andes in the Bible-world, and make men look at them. One good look at Mont Blanc—why, it is worth a voyage to Europe! The great sculptors of Greece did not lay out their strength on carving cherry-stones. They toiled on Jupiters, Apollos, and Minervas. Now, ministers often pass by the great facts, and the rich, succulent texts, perhaps because others, perhaps because they, have preached on them years ago, and they conclude the people remembered them as well as the preachers. But they do not in point of fact (their minds have not, indeed, been refreshed by occasional glances at the manuscripts), and if they did, let there be new sermons on them, with new views, or new feelings, or new illustrations, and ordinarily there will be some new hearers to be instructed.

4. Have an aim in each sermon. Do not enter on it because you *must preach something*. If any one should say to you, What are you driving at? you should have no hesitation in answering. Let there be, for example, one great truth, of which you give the evidence, the elucidation, and the application, or one great duty of which you give the obligation and the best helps you can to its performance. Direct your arrows at objects without being personal; come near your hearers. Letters dropped into the post-office without address go to the dead-letter office, and are of no use to anybody.

This distinct, definite aim will give, what all writers emphasize (Cicero not the least forcibly), namely, unity. So much has been written on it that I do not formally include it. I find, moreover, that early Christian preachers have often disregarded the received rules of rhetoric on this subject; and yet, I dare say, they had—or they could not have been the good preachers they were—definite aims which gave a real, though not a formal, unity to their discourses. The young sermon-writer wishes to be full, and fearing paucity of truths at the end, crowds in all he knows pertinent to the subject at the beginning. It is as if he had to write a description of New Haven, and distrusting his store of materials, he dwells so long on the meadows and their heaps of hay on stilts, shrinking from the soil that bore them, that he has not time for the noble spaces, the elms, the edifices, and the material for one of the finest university quadrangles in the world. But thought, observation, experience, and especially fullness of mind, will correct this error, and a man will find out that he is to be sure of his target, and his bullet, and that he is to use no unnecessary powder.

5. Consider the time, place, and other conditions as affecting yourselves, and the people, in the preparation of your sermons. There would be some incongruity, for example, in one of you, during the first year of your ministry, announcing as a text, "I have been young and now I am old," etc.* Admitting the propriety of your enforcing the truth of that verse, texts can be found that would not make any one smile as you read them. There are portions of God's Word which pastors long settled, and settled in the esteem and regard of their people, may well preach from, which yet would lose their force in an occasional sermon. Such a text is, "My little children, of whom I travail in birth again," etc. †

The circumstances of the people addressed are to be carefully studied. I will be forgiven for marking here what I am deeply convinced accounts for the failure of many ministers. They are called to quiet, retired charges, among plain people. They look higher for their future spheres of labor. So the

---

* Ps. xxxvii. 25.   † Gal. iv. 19.

sermons they write are not exclusively, not even mainly, for their present lowly charge, but for a cultivated, numerous, and appreciative city audience, which at present exists only in their imagination: perhaps never does anywhere else. For, assuredly, the best way for a man to get out of a lowly position is to be conspicuously effective in it. I am assured by your Professors that nothing can be more welcome than any bit of personal experience, and that its employment here will be warranted by the object in view. I was selected, while in the senior year of my course, by my fellow-students to be their missionary in an outpost, where the congregation consisted of about eighty or ninety persons, one-tenth of them, say, cultivated, another tenth fairly intelligent, and the rest poor, ignorant peasants, speaking English imperfectly. I had, happily, only two sermons from my class exercises, of which I did not conceive highly. I have them still in reserve for a very rainy day. I was licensed on a Tuesday, and reached my field on Thursday night. I began on the next Lord's day. I knew my people's condition, and I wrote my sermon on Saturday. If these poor people were to understand me at all, I must be simple. If they were to be kept listening, I must go rapidly from thought to thought. There must be what Cicero, Horace, and all the rhetorical authorities (I know now, I did not then), call *movement*. If they are to see my points, illustrations from their own line of observation must make them vivid; and yet, if there is anything coarse, vulgar, tawdry, or puerile, the good taste and feeling of the cultivated will be offended. For such a congregation for the first two or three years of my life I prepared and preached my sermons. I got other like congregations all around on weekdays. The floor on which I stood was often earthen, the roof not frescoed, the pulpit not ecclesiastical; but I state a simple fact when I say that many of the sermons I prepared for that people I have repeated in New York, with apparent attention and profit on the part of the people. Is that because I had New York in my mind's eye when writing them? No, indeed! It is because I had topics of great, worldwide, and everlasting interest. They were, and are, reàl, living, all-momentous truths to me. I got into the way of making them as plain as I could to the people I was bound to teach, *and it was the best possible preparation for me for the work of making them as plain as I can to the people I am bound to teach now.* Gentlemen, wherever God puts you, do the best you can for the people there, as if you were to live and die among them. Any duties a man does with a view to something else remote and different, he is apt to do in a perfunctory and ineffective way. If you are a minister or missionary of a small company, with an income of five hundred dollars—which is more than I began on—do your very best for that company; and if you grow, and it is best for you, the Lord will send somebody in search of you for a greater; for there is no waste of power in His well-ordered kingdom.

6. There is an indescribable but quite real gain to a preacher arising out of his own sympathy with his subject. A man will write and speak with languor and feebleness on Christian joy and gladness, if his own spirit is depressed; and he will usually feel a corresponding embarrassment in discussing spiritual depression, its causes and cure, if he is himself in exuberant spirits. I leave out of account, of course, men who carry into the pulpit the faculties and powers of the actor, and even those who have such facility of adaptation that for the time they com-

pletely throw themselves into the required rôle. I speak of ordinary, truthful, sincere men. This circumstance should be taken into account in the choice of subjects. Some regard is to be had to your own mental and spiritual condition. Whether a man should ever speak above and beyond his own experience is a question on which I do not enter here; but for his own sake, his people's sake, and the sake of the sermon, he should have his theme as far as possible in the current of his own thoughts and feelings. There are topics, indeed, as to which this will only become the case by effort, by contact with others, and by prayer. If a week has been marked, for example, by sickness and death among the people, then the sermon may well catch its spirit from the state of mind thus induced. I think it a dangerous thing to one's self to deliver, with any amount of feeling evoked by the occasion, the sublime truths of revelation, without a present, immediate sympathy with them. I should fear its effect in hardening the heart, producing insincerity, and blunting the perceptions. Now, this temptation can be reduced by choosing themes so far in accord with the tone of your own minds that no violence will be done them in the discussion, and that the preaching will be congenial work, and enlist your whole faculties. Of course, this may be put in another fashion: be spiritually-minded; live much in the written Word of God; be in sympathy with the Incarnate Word, and you will be at home among the themes of which the Bible speaks, and you are to discourse. And in connection with this, live much among your people. It has sometimes happened to me to be away during the week, and to return at the end of it for the Sabbath. It may seem absurd to you, but I have often set out on the Saturday afternoon to make two or three calls among my people to renew and fix the sense that they belonged to me, and I to them, in order to comfort in the services of the following Lord's Day.

And now, as to the actual making of the sermon, its theme being chosen with due regard to the conditions stated, no one man can lay down rules for another. This much, however, in general terms, I do not hesitate to say to you, while you are young men and young ministers, *write your sermons with the utmost care.* Write with the most lucid order you can secure. Write in the best language, the most concise, elegant, and transparent you can command.

Write in the most correct and faultless style your judgment approves. Write every word, or an equivalent for every word, and set down every idea you ought to give to the people, and in its relative place. Write, if necessary, more than once, first a brief, then a *precis* of greater length, then a full and complete presentation of the whole matter as you are to give it to the people. I say this to you with the utmost explicitness, and with the strongest emphasis. Forego every bottle but the ink-bottle. Write regularly, conscientiously, and at your best. I urge this on you all the more because I am myself described, in a way that may mislead, as an *extempore* speaker, and I should be extremely vexed if my supposed method should ensnare any one into the delusion that any purely *extempore* plan is likely to be permanently effective with ordinary men. Whether you take your manuscript to the pulpit, or burn it when you have done your best upon it, or leave it in some *limbus sermonum* to be be burned by ungrateful posterity, is of secondary, that you write is of the first, importance.

If you inquire why this is urged so vehemently, let me reply succinctly. It is the way to prune off redundancies. It is the way to exactness of phraseology. It is the best method of taking one's own measure. One has an idea, or a group of them, by which he is impressed. They loom large. Like the stars in the sky, they appear numerous from their very lack of order. He thinks himself rich. He has his mental picture of them, and they move over the landscape of his imagination like the bits of glass in a kaleidoscope. He sits down to put them on paper. One, two, three—what's the matter? Where are all the rest? There are not so many as he thought; and, behold, they are—now that he looks at them on paper—not so brilliant as he imagined. They do not sparkle. There is no corruscation. If he is to make a display, he must get more thoughts and other images! Had he got on his feet with just those pieces, he must have kept the kaleidoscope in constant motion, showing always the same bits of glass, only in somewhat different combinations.

When a man writes his sermon as well as he can, he has a kind of outward and sensible sign to himself of honest preparation. He is stronger for it. He cannot write down what he feels to be absolute nonsense. Self-respect forbids his wasting good paper on mere truisms, on absolute commonplace, and needless repetition. If there is anything in him he will bring it out and put it on paper. If there is not, the paper will help him to see it, and the sooner he does, the better, for human "nature abhors a vacuum."

At a later stage I shall tell you how all this is compatible with a free delivery of one's thoughts, and, if it interests any one, shall state my own method. But here I am anxious to combat the objections that will arise in some minds to this writing plan. "Lawyers and legislators do not write." How do you know? On the contrary, the very best legal speakers have been sedulous, painstaking writers, often rewriting, revising, altering, and amending. You tell me of old and experienced Senators who, in the nature of the case, cannot write replies to speeches made on the spot. Ah, yes! but we are not talking of old and experienced Senators, but of young and quite inexperienced ministers. And even with the Senators, the case differs from ours. A question is up for a month at a time. It is discussed at the table, in the lobbies, in the smoking-room, and in all the papers. A man is talking of little else while the thing is on the carpet. When he gets on his feet, he has only to marshal in order what has been on his lips, and in his brain for long, and in which thought has been stimulated by all the contact of mind with mind. And then, bear in your thoughts, that when that matter is issued, it is gone; and there is no such temptation to go back and quote himself as there would be if he had to discourse twice on the same theme, or a branch of it, on Sabbath, and on one week night, all the year round.

It is true you can point to eminent men who do not write; and one who nobly fills a foremost place in the pulpit has conspicuously discarded paper. But that is after a quarter of a century of writing; and it is accompanied by the caution that one is still to write, for the reasons given already, only not what you are preaching. Whenever a kind Providence fills theological seminaries with men of the ripe culture, ready fluency, calm equipoise, and copious knowledge, of that eminent brother, aided by a quarter of a century of most effective writing, then and not till then the amateur Professor—like myself—of that day, may counsel the abandonment of the writing. But is it fair to belittle the ladder by which we climbed?

You may point indeed to effective speeches, made "on the spur of the moment;" but they are no argument in the case. There was something—a scene, an opponent, an argument, that drew them forth. But, Gentlemen, we cannot get up a stimulating scene, in God's house, three times a week. And if you had an honest opinion from those who did so well on the spur of the moment, you would commonly find that faithful memory, put on her mettle, reproduced something laid up before, in perhaps another connection, and for another purpose. I have heard many speeches, of various degrees of merit, in all sorts of circumstances; and it has been my own lot to make several, mostly of little account; and my deliberate opinion is, that hardly anything is of value that has not been prepared, and prepared for the occasion of delivery.

On the subject of divisions of sermons, of the relations of exordium, exposition, proposition, main argument, and conclusion, or peroration, on which Aristotle, Cicero, Quinctilian and Horace have written, I do not dwell. There are three books in which these topics are discussed at length, and to advantage, all within your reach, and which you can study at your leisure—only do not put it off, for you will get little leisure when you are pastors—namely Whately's, *Rhetoric*, Dr. Dabney's *Sacred Rhetoric*, and the volume on the "*Office and Work of the Christian Ministry*," * than which I have seen no more exact and adequate text-book. In specifying these I am not to be understood as depreciating the various excellencies of Campbell, Porter, Shedd, Vinet, or the admirable "Thoughts on Preaching" of my predecessor in New York, which, unhappily, he did not live to set in order with the consummate taste with which his works are finished.

I will only add in conclusion, Gentlemen, that when a sermon has been written, full of matter, clear in order, vivid in illustration, rapid and graceful in movement, evangelical in tone, and fitted to the best of your ability to the people who are to hear it, whether you read or utter its thoughts, one more element in preparation is not to be omitted—for if omitted your other toil goes for little. "The flesh profiteth nothing," nor eloquence, nor imagination, nor demonstration, even of inspired truth. "It is the

---

* "OFFICE AND WORK OF THE CHRISTIAN MINISTRY," by James M. Hoppin, Professor of Homiletics and Pastoral Theology in Yale College.

spirit that quickeneth." Take your sermon, lay it out before God your Saviour and Master, make it a clear offering to Him. Say to Him, "Here, Lord, I am Thine; for Thee, and for none other. This is Thy truth. I have done my utmost to set it forth in order. Lord take it; use it; help me to be nothing, to forget myself, my work, my effort, and let the people see only Thee, hear only Thy word, deal only with Thee, that beholding Thy beauty, they may love Thee, that seeing Thine image they may be changed into it, by the Spirit of God."

Having seen your dimness in His great light, and felt your feebleness in presence of His power, commit your work to Him, and let there be, if possible, no more of self blending with it. Go and preach, now. No matter how you are criticised; no matter how weak you seem when you have preached.* The

---

* It is difficult to get rid of the idea that preachers who have acquired some position, and become objects of popular notice, become less useful as preachers in their high, than in their lower, estate. While a man is pursuing his work unnoticed and comparatively unknown, he usually does it in the way he finds best for results, and with little regard to rules. But the moment he becomes a little prominent, the vultures are gathered together. From the secular, and, more vulgar and vulgarizing still, from the religious press, literary scouts are detached to scrutinize, and

Lord's word has had free course: and it is His way by the weak things of the world to confound the mighty. He stains the pride of all human glory, that according as it is written "he that glorieth, let him glory in the Lord." Now, it is no matter if there be opposition. It is not against you—you are no longer in the case. The soul has heard the Lord. He will take care of His work and glory.

> "Faint not, and fret not, for threatened woe,
>   Watchman on Truth's gray height!
> Few though the faithful, and fierce though the foe.
>   Weakness is aye Heaven's might.
>
> Time's years are many, Eternity one,
>   And one is the Infinite;
> The chosen are few, few the deeds well done,
>   For scantness is still heaven's might."

---

report " how he does it ; " as if he were an actor, trained to play his part, and as fair a subject for discussion as if every man had paid his dollar for the opportunity to witness his tricks of rhetoric. His figure, his dress, his hair, his pronunciation, his height, the plans on which they suppose he proceeds (when in most cases he has no plans), are all duly set forth, with a fullness and accuracy proportioned to the invention and power of observation of the critics. Gentlemen! we are not on exhibition. We are trying to do a solemn duty, under great responsibilities. To keep down self-consciousness and forget ourselves is one of our hardest tasks, if you will but think of it. Do not, please, make it harder for us.

LECTURE VI.

A PILE of cannon-balls on the grass, uniform, round, shining, heavy, may represent a pile of sermons. They are sometimes heavy also—not in the military sense. But as with the bullets, much of their efficacy will depend on the aim, the force, and the general manner of delivery. Many sermons are fired too high, many are misdirected, many fall short of the mark, or, like spent bullets, they do little execution. We propose to devote the most of this hour to the question of delivering sermons.

To avoid disappointment at the close, let it be stated here that the lecturer knows no secret of success, has no uniform rule that infallibly succeeds, and does not believe there is such a rule in existence. The trees, as they were made, bring forth fruit after their kind, and all that gardeners can do is to give them a fair field, and keep off all noxious things.

1. Some read their sermons word for word as written, from beginning to end. The extent to which this practice prevails is so great as to make it certain that it cannot be absurd and ridiculous on its face. Many, perhaps the great majority, of the English Episcopal clergy do this. So do many of the Presbyterian clergy in Scotland. So do most of the Congregational, Baptist, Presbyterian, and Episcopal clergy, I presume, of America. Not only is this the case, but many of the very greatest preachers, like Jonathan Edwards in this country, like Chalmers in Scotland, read their sermons. The advantages are many. Precision, exactness, and freedom from all offensive excrescences, such as loose language, colloquialisms, disjointed grammar, and rambling repetition, are, or ought to be, secured. Brevity is also more easily arranged for and assured. There is also a fair presumption established in the mind of the hearer that the preacher has made preparation, for there is the manuscript before him. In England this presumption is weakened in a good degree by the known traffic in sermons, and by incidents, grave

and gay, of which every one has heard, as to sermons that have done more than double duty. One of the greatest gains, it appears to me, is found in the closeness and consecutiveness of thought, and the felicity of expression, which it is difficult to have but by the reading of written composition. I confess that when I have occasionally listened to the better order of preachers of this type, and have noticed the faultless and elegant diction, and the charm of ornate composition, pleasing as it strikes the ear, I have had moments of despair, and thought how absurd and unreasonable it is to expect such audiences to listen to any one who adopts the plan to which I have been led, and which must necessarily lack these attractive peculiarities.

But there are considerations on the other side. A directness of address is attainable in another way, which it is difficult to have in reading. The emotion of yesterday cannot always be at the call of the preacher when he reads, as when he wrote, though it must be admitted that genuine pathos or genuine humor will affect when read, no matter when written; the jokes, therefore, over "feelings a week old" have no adequate foundation. The number of men who can, or do, read so well as to turn attention from the reading, and fix it on the person and the ideas, is, unfortunately, not large. Nor does it certainly follow that a man has given a matter thorough and effective preparation because he has written. There is extempore writing, as truly as extempore speaking.

This much, then, must be admitted, that while many are most effective and admirable when reading sermons, there is nothing in the nature of things to make it the absolute rule, and it has some inherent disadvantages to be got over. This further observation may be made, that they who read ought to read well, that is, with distinctness; enough loudness to be audible without effort from the hearers; with proper emphasis; and with suitable feeling. And yet, if the reading be obviously artistic, it offends. Good reading, like a good style in writing, should be like clear glass, of which the eye takes no account because it perfectly sees through it the objects beyond. All the ornamental in reading or in writing is like the colors on stained glass. What is gained in beauty is lost in transparency.

2. A second method is employed by those who

write and then commit to memory, and repeat to the audience. Many Scotch preachers begin and go through life on this plan, acquiring a certain facility of remembering, after some time, by which the early labor is greatly reduced. On this method, onlookers may draw conclusions from general principles which are not borne out by fact. It might be thought, for example, an almost impossible thing to learn a sermon of an hour, and perhaps two of them for a day. It might be thought that the mind would be so busy in remembering, as to have no time for feeling. It might be thought that action, and all other concomitants of natural communication, would be necessarily shut out by the one absorbing effort to get the ideas and words into their places. Yet, in point of fact, these evils are escaped by the best preachers of this sort. They do feel, and show feeling; do move eye and hand and body in sympathy with their words, and produce, as in his line an actor does, as a good elocutionist does, great effects by their efforts. I think it likely that Whitfield did not write; but he had gone over a certain set of truths and remarks until they were as good as written. The same is true, I presume, of a living American

Evangelist, who is now preaching in Great Britain with very marked blessing. No one who has gone through an American college can miss knowing the steps of the process; for all stage-speaking is done in this way; and many men never make as much impression as orators in all their future life as in their "pieces" on the stage. If they were obliged to write more and more speeches, memorize, and deliver them, the exercise would become easier, and many men who now read would thus be more effective than on their present method.

Yet, it must be admitted that there are considerations on the other side. Some are deficient in verbal memory. Some are incapable of trusting themselves. Some are so obviously and completely introverted—the eye on vacancy, the brow contracted, and the perplexed and distracted mind running to and fro in the chambers of the brain, looking for missing words, searching in the dark, very much like Æneas when calling again and again for the lost Creusa! And the same want of spontaneity, freshness, and directness chargeable on the reading plan is, in a degree, to be expected here. Yet, we repeat, evils which we, in theory, might expect are, by many, avoided in actual practice, for the human mind is a wonderful instrument, and capable of astonishing adaptations.

They who make addresses on this plan, have especial need to cultivate the voice, or it is in great danger of becoming a monotone. The air of average church-buildings, particularly in the afternoons and evenings, co-operating with the mental and bodily condition of many hearers, is so conducive to sleep, that it is undesirable to invite "tired nature's sweet restorer" by the voice in the pulpit. When both eye-gate and ear-gate are closed "the city of Mansoul," as Bunyan represents it, cannot be entered for its good. To speak naturally, even what we have ourselves written, is difficult; yet not, it seems to me, quite so difficult as to read naturally. A larger proportion, according to my observation, of readers than of non-readers, suffer from weakened throats. This may be explained in part by the fact that in reading the head is bent; there is a pressure on the vocal organs, which work at a disadvantage as compared with the ease and freedom they enjoy in an erect speaker. In the Episcopal Church the reading of the service, if followed by sermons by the same men, such as are preached elsewhere, would become intolerable, and, in point of fact, breaks down many who attempt it. The good preachers usually have readers.

3. The third method is that which almost every one has adopted some time or other, namely, the making of a brief with heads, divisions, and catchwords on which the eye rests, while the mind is expected to find suitable language on the occasion. It is a very common, and very effective plan with many, notwithstanding its alleged resemblance to a chicken stooping for a mouthful of water, and then stretching up the neck to get the benefit of it and send it to its proper place. A man who finds he can manage very well on this plan, ought, it seems to me, to be at the pains sometime to fix in his mind the entries on his bit of paper, and dispense with it, and at least ascertain by experience, if an increase of power be not within his reach.

From having employed this plan for many years in a ladies' class of between two and three hundred persons, and where many Scripture texts are in requisition, I know that it can be harmonized with considerable freedom of speech. Still, a man must know his subject thoroughly, or there will be bondage, and the chains will clank.

4. The fourth and last method is to prepare what one has to say with care and exactness, in the substance and the words, so as to have it all before the mind, and then to stand up and give the sense of it to the people, in such language as comes at the moment. The mode of preparation may be by writing, or, as it is in, I think, exceptional cases, without writing, but solely by meditation. In harmony with what has been said already, and from my own experience, I think the writing is better than the mere meditation for ordinary men.

I am assured that there will be pardon extended to me for the egotism of detailing here my own experience. I wrote, and in a sort of way, memorized two or three class exercises when a student. I had to preach before the Presbytery, and it was the custom for each minister to criticise. One good, wise, and plain-spoken man remarked that "the young man seemed to look only at some object in the corner of the gallery, and, moreover, to be very much afraid of it. He ought to look at those to whom he speaks." That was a true and a salutary criticism. I laid it to heart; I never tried memorizing again. From that time and onward I put on paper all I knew about my subject, in the order in which it had better be spoken. I fix this order and the illustrations in my mind, in studious disregard of the language, except in the case of definitions, if there are any, depending on verbal exactness. I try to have it so that I could talk it over; give the end first, or begin in the middle if need be, and then I go to the pulpit, and converse with the people about the matter in a tone loud enough to be heard through the house, if I can. That is all. There is no secret about it, Gentlemen.

Some inquisitive person may ask how long this fixing process requires? The time varies; but this rule is pretty uniform—the worse the sermon, the longer it takes. A good sermon has points, natural divisions, inherent helps to memory. It is like a New England village, each house with something distinctive about it. A poor sermon is like a street of brown stone houses, all much alike in dull monotony in everything but the numbers, which usually (so perverse is human nature) you can only see by climbing the stoop.

When a good sermon is finished on Saturday, a

reading that evening, and another, more hurried, on Sabbath morning, is sufficient, and a couple of hours is quite enough to repossess one's self of the right kind of sermon written twenty years ago.

Now, one may say, why take the trouble to write? Already general considerations on that subject have been submitted, to which it is sufficient here to refer. For me, I should not feel that I had done my utmost without it. I have an indefinite feeling that the sermon written is a tangible property, common to me and to my people. I see just how much I know, and how much I can hope to make the people know. If I cannot put an idea down on paper, so that I can tell it intelligibly to the people, then it might do for a book, but it does not suit a sermon. I cannot expect the people to remember what I could not. So the composition comes to have a tacit, constant reference to the speaking, and the ideas and illustrations take on a kind of fitness for conversational use, and though the outcome will often lack neatness, exactness, delicacy of touch, and sustained elevation, it is a part of myself, and I have the feeling that it may and can become a part of my hearers.

I have already repeatedly, and I hope sufficiently,

guarded myself against being supposed to dictate to each man the way in which he is to preach, irrespective of habits, temperament, and aptitudes. For the sake of those who are considering how they are to proceed in the formation of their plans, it may be proper here to state a few considerations, in favor of what I shall call *accurate writing and free delivery.*

It must be owned that the reading of sermons is unknown in the reports that come to us of apostolic preaching. The apostles spake " boldly " (*parresia*), with freedom of speech (Acts iv. 13); and a picture of any one of them reading an address to the people would be instantly challenged as palpably inaccurate. The same is true of our Lord, not only in His discourses to the people by the sea-side and the way-side, but in His exposition in the synagogue. He closed the book, and gave it to the minister, and sat down; and when the expectant looks of the people invited an address, " he began to say unto them." (Luke iv. 20, 21.)

Now, it may be alleged that these cases are not in point, on two grounds: that in the first place the sermons of that time were not the formal, didactic statements now required, but personal narratives, or arguments made and sustained by quotation from the Divine Word, as in the case of Peter's preaching at Pentecost; and in the second place, these preachers certainly did not write sermons, but spoke, in the literal sense of the phrase, *extempore*.

As to the former of these two rejoinders, it is freely admitted that apostolic addresses were informal and undetermined by any homiletical rules for sermon-making. But it will be remembered that we plead for a return to their method; for a less restrained plan; for the opening up of the Scriptures, in the form of exposition. So far we should bring ourselves into closer accord with the apostolic ministry. It would be gratuitous to assume that when Paul opened his mouth on Mars' Hill to preach to sophists and idolaters, he had made no preparation. He could not move among images and altars without reflection on the specific truth which was to overthrow both the one and the other. His mind was too active to allow him to gaze in unreflecting wonder. But when he did speak, his sermon was obviously born of the occasion; drew its force and inspiration from the surroundings; and had all the freedom and impetus of a decided, prompt utterance from a well-furnished head and a fervent heart.

That they did not write is to be accounted for in part by the supernatural aid given to them; and in part by the occasional character of their ministrations. They moved from place to place in most cases, and do not stand in the same relation as the settled pastor.

There is another form of authority on this subject which I do not remember to have seen adduced, and yet which, it seems to me, is admissible. It is common and just to say that the later prophets of the Old Testament constituted a providential preparation for the New Testament. As one reads through his Bible in order, the priest becomes of less and less importance, and the teacher rises into prominence. Quite early in Hebrew history, theological seminaries have a place, and the "sons of the prophets" occupied them, receiving instruction in music and the sacred Scriptures. The far-seeing patriots of Israel, like Elijah and Elisha, saw the need of an educated body of instructors for the people, if Baal-worship was to be excluded. Now, the inspired prophets, who, as a rule, were of this class, but rendered pre-eminent by inspiration, according to my conception of their work, delivered the messages, as the word of the Lord, to the people, not always, indeed, comprehending the tidings they bore, but employing their own minds on them, as we do on the Bible; and their written statements remain as the permanent record of their fidelity, and the means of warning and instruction to all future ages. According to this conception, there is little difficulty in accounting for the abrupt transitions, the frequent changes of person, of scenery, and of style of address. We have in our hands, in fact, the written communications which they, putting themselves into the right state of mental receptivity, obtained from the Lord, and which they made the basis of addresses to the people. In so far (and only in so far, for there are many obvious differences) they seem to me to furnish example to us of lowly, prayerful waiting on God, in the study of His word, and in careful preparation, followed by free, earnest spoken address to the people. Nor can we do any better than they did in that time of genuine revival described in 2 Chron. xvii. 9, when Levites and priests "taught in Judah, and had the book of the law of the Lord with them, and went about throughout all the cities of Judah, and taught the people. And the fear of the Lord fell upon all the kingdoms of the lands that were round about Judah, so that they made no war against Jehoshaphat." Now, as then, a strong and faithful pulpit is no mean safeguard of a nation's life.

For four or five centuries after our Lord's ascension the ordinary preaching was mainly expository, and delivered without notes; but if we may draw a conclusion from the homilies, commentaries, and other works that remain, written preparation was made. The same was true in much later times: hence the voluminous remains of many preachers. If any of you look with amazement on the immense amount of printed matter left by some of the Reformers and some of the Puritans, remember two things; the less important, that these worthy men were not required to keep abreast of a religious press like ours, and read numerous newspapers and pamphlets, nor to attend interminable meetings and committees, the excrescences on modern Christian life in which Christian activity is organized away to so large an extent, out of the hands of individuals. The second and more important is that they habitually expounded the word of God, and that we have nearly all that they wrote and spoke.*

It was with the admission into the church of the method of the schools that the simplicity, naturalness, and directness of the early preaching were exchanged for formal methods, excessively minute analysis, and multitudinous divisions, of which it has been wittily said that, like the bones in Ezekiel's valley of vision, "there were very many—and they were very dry." So soon as men began to make, as Nathaniel Hardy does, fifty-nine sermons on the first and second chapters of 1st John, being earnest and evangelical, anx-

---

* In Nichols' Series of Commentaries, issued in Edinburgh some years ago, is the well-known work, "A COMMENTARY ON THE WHOLE EPISTLE TO THE HEBREWS. Being the substance of thirty years' Wednesday's Lectures at Blackfriars, London, by that holy and learned divine, William Gouge, D.D., and late Pastor there." An account of his life and labors is prefixed, which ministers would do well to read in these times of apparent overwork, when they are tempted to think no lot so hard as their own. Gouge was a model pastor, and his Wednesday lectures had such a place in the public esteem "that when the godly Christians of those times came out of the country into London, they thought not their business done unless they had been at Blackfriars Lecture."

ious to tell the saving truth, they are tempted to strain passages in order to get in all they desire, and so they become less accurate than they should be in reflecting the mind of the Spirit and nothing more, in the Scriptures discussed.

But, in the next place, is there not a form in which the help of the Holy Ghost may be realized, where a man has put down, for the sake of accuracy, and in the way of honest preparation, what he feels he ought to teach, and then expects, as to the delivery, that it will be given him in that hour what he shall say? Dr. Parker* makes a distinction between interpretation, which usually comes slowly as the fruit of labor and diligence (though a meaning may suddenly flash out to the eye of a devout and attentive reader), and the utterance of the interpretation. No man is at liberty to go into the pulpit and count on the instant help of the Holy Ghost to interpret to him the Divine Word. By its very nature the Bible is in his hand; he can study it at leisure. The Lord does not supersede human diligence by supernatural aid. No need exists to wait for the public

---

*THE PARACLETE (p. 89), New York: Scribner, Armstrong & Co.

occasion, to ascertain its meaning. That can be done in the closet. But he thinks it is different with utterance. The public occasion changes conditions, introduces electric sympathy, brings high excitement, and intense emotion. Memory, fancy, and especially feeling, are stimulated. This is all confessedly on the human side, but Dr. Parker thinks that it cannot be offensive to the Holy Ghost to ask such power of utterance—not literary finish, or the conditions of successful authorship—as will effectively reach the human heart. All this, it must be admitted, will apply also to writing, "so that it shall reach the heart." So far Dr. Parker's argument seems to me to prove nothing in favor of his plan, unless, indeed, it could be shown that reading preachers do not honor the Holy Ghost by asking guidance in writing, which is absurd. But he does raise a good point in another connection, namely, that what a man has written in "cool blood in his study, and which he reads *verbatim*, cannot have the help which a congregation affords to the urgent, rapid, percussive, and living utterance that cannot be printed." *

---

* The Paraclete, p. 90.

All that can be said, probably, on the subject, is that when a minister is convinced in his judgment that he can effect more by speaking than reading his sermons, and, at any cost of trouble or anxiety, determines to do it, he may rely on the Holy Ghost for aid, just as in any other duty which is difficult, and yet not to be evaded. And I think, in the matter of words, he will usually receive that aid. He may not necessarily be an eloquent or a successful preacher, in the common, popular acceptation; but one thing you will learn, Gentlemen, in the course of your Christian life, that men are very fallible judges of our success. All too often "that which is highly esteemed among men is abomination in the sight of God." *

In the next place, some importance is to be attached to the views and experience of those who have rendered good service as preachers. So far as there is evidence on the subject, it is plain that in the days of great patristic preaching, some variety of method obtained, as at present. Some read wholly; some memorized; some prepared material before-

---

* Luke xvi. 15.

hand; some literally extemporized, finding the topic in the passage read, or in a passing incident connected with the service. The Presbyters made exhortations, and their President followed in a longer discourse. This we learn from the *Apostolical Constitutions*, so called.* But the life of true religion had so entirely run into rubric and ritual, as it is shadowed to us in the *Constitutions*, that little weight can be attached thereto.

Probably Chrysostom and Augustine, widely differing in style and in substance, would be commonly regarded as the best preachers of their age. Both

---

* It is not necessary to remind most readers that these literary remains are not of the Apostles, though ostentatiously claiming to be, describing the "Acts of the Apostles," as "our Acts." Bunsen thinks they reflect the life of the Church of the second and third centuries. The translation best known is Whiston's. Believing them to be "the most sacred of the canonical books of the New Testament," he has, of course, given them an extremely rubrical tone, such as would delight the heart of a *very* High-Churchman, if, indeed, they did not sometimes go too far, as in inculcating the kiss as a part of the service. In all likelihood it will be found that an early directory for worship has been interpolated to suit the condition of things growing up in the fourth and fifth centuries, when "priest," "sacrifice," and even a peculiar dress for the deacon were familiar to the Christians. See Book II., § VII., ch. 58.

were expository. Both prepared carefully at home. Both spoke to the people. Augustine could never have preached ten sermons in five days, as he frequently did, on any other plan. Both were careful in their exegesis, with such appliances as they enjoyed. Both reached at once the most cultivated and the most common intellects. Both made the basis of their teaching Scriptural, and both were able to effect in their mode of working much more, as far as we can see, than in our modern methods of sermonizing.

The era of the Middle Ages is, as far as preaching is concerned, a wilderness resounding with the cries of sacerdotal parrots, and relieved only by the monkey tricks of fanatical friars. No language compatible with conventional propriety could describe the degradation of that time. No wonder that Luther, who broke through and broke up this state of things, is sometimes harsh and coarse. The wonder is, that he is so measured.

But to the point immediately in hand. It is not too much to say that the greatest preachers of Germany were expository, and were speakers, not readers. The same is true of the French, the Scottish, the English pulpit, even in its two sections—Non

Conformist and Episcopal. Hooker did not read. The great Puritans spoke after careful preparation; so did the early fathers of the New England churches,* as a rule. The same is true of the great masters of pulpit eloquence nearer to our own time, such as John M. Mason, of this country, and Robert Hall, of England. They broke away from the cold, philosophic matter, and the neat moralities appropriately dressed in blameless English, of which Paley and Blair were the types. I have not so high an estimate of Frederick Robertson as a teacher, as many others; but his attractiveness as a preacher was great. His sermons, like the late Dr. Guthrie's and Mr. Spurgeon's, were spoken after careful, though (in his case) not written preparation. It would be unfair to omit, on the other side, that Chalmers read, and Candlish, for the most part.

When I had no more idea of being in the pulpit of Dr. James W. Alexander than of being in the

---

* From a valuable painting in the possession of R. L. Stuart, Esq., of New York, presumably accurate, they also wore gown and bands, and that when they walked to church in the wilderness, guarded by armed men, each carrying his firelock and his Bible.

7*

Cabinet, I procured his *Thoughts on Preaching*. The following passage, commending, as the result of thought, the plan on which, substantially, I had been working, without any thought, afforded me immense encouragement :

"If you press me to say which is absolutely the best practice in regard to 'notes,' properly so called, that is, in distinction from a complete manuscript, I unhesitatingly say, USE NONE. Carry no scrap of writing into the pulpit. Let your scheme, with all its branches, be written on your mental tablet. The practice will be invaluable. I know a public speaker about my age who has never employed a note of any kind. But while this is a counsel for which, if you follow it, you will thank me as long as you live, I am pretty sure you have not courage and self-denial to make the venture. And I admit that some great preachers have been less vigorous. The late Mr. Wirt, himself one of the most classical and brilliant extempore orators of America, used to speak in admiration of his pastor, the beloved Nevins, of Baltimore. Now, having often counseled with this eloquent clergyman, I happen to know that while his morning discourses were committed to memory, his afternoon discourses were from a 'brief.' A greater orator than either, who was at the same time a friend of both, thus advised a young preacher: 'In your case,' said Summerfield, 'I would recommend the choice of a companion or two, with whom you could accustom yourself to open and amplify your thoughts on a portion of the word of God in the way of lecture. Choose a copious subject, and be not anxious to say all that might be said. Let your efforts be aimed at giving a strong outline; the filling-up will be much more easily attained. Prepare a skeleton of your leading ideas, branching them off into their secondary relations. This you may have before you. Digest well the subject, but be not careful to choose your *words* previous to your delivery. Follow out the idea with such language as may offer at the moment. Don't be discouraged if you fall down a hundred times; for though you fall you shall rise again; and cheer yourself with the prophet's challenge, "Who hath despised the day of small things?"' If any words of mine could be needed to reinforce the opinion of the most enchanting speaker I ever heard, I should employ them in fixing in your mind the counsel *not to prepare your words.* Certain preachers, by a powerful and constraining discipline, have acquired the faculty of mentally rehearsing the entire discourse which they were to deliver, with almost the precise language. This is manifestly no more extemporaneous preaching than if they had written down every word in a book. It is almost identical with what is called *memoriter* preaching. But if you would avail yourself of the plastic power of excitement in a great assembly to create for the gushing thought a mold of fitting diction, you will not spend a moment on the words, following Horace :

' Verbaque *provisam* rem non invita sequentur.

"Nothing more effectually ruffles that composure of mind which the preacher needs, than to have a disjointed train of half-remembered words floating in the mind. For which reason few persons have ever been successful in a certain method which I have seen proposed, to wit: that the young speaker should prepare his manuscript, give it a thorough reading beforehand, and then preach with a general recollection of its contents. The result is that the mind is in a libration and pother, betwixt the word in the paper and the probably better word which comes to the tip of the tongue. Generally speaking, the best possible word is the one which is born of the thought in the presence of the assembly. And the less you think about words as a separate affair, the better they will be. My sedulous endeavor is then to carry your attention back to the great earnest business of conveying God's message to the soul; being convinced that here as elsewhere the seeking of God's kingdom and righteousness will best secure subordinate matters."

I only add that the estimates of the relative values of plans must vary with education and habit. When the author of the "Burial of Sir John Moore" was a curate in a small parish in the North of Ireland, the Presbyterians used to hear him with pleasure in the evening, their highest commendation of him being that "he preached like a meeting minister." On the other hand, in many places of New England and America generally, a man is not thought worth hearing who does not read his sermon. Could a compromise be effected on the plan suggested in the following anecdote? A leading Welsh minister—and Welsh ministers are, I think, among the best preachers—was invited to preach an anniversary sermon before one of the great societies in London. Naturally anxious to disregard no propriety, he consulted the proper authority, the secretary. "Should I read my sermon?" "Oh, it is no matter; only bring some of your Welsh fire with you." "But you cannot, my dear sir, carry fire in paper." "No, that is true; but you may use the paper to kindle the fire!"

LECTURE VII.

We have now reached the point where we can raise the question, What, practically, are the characteristics of a good sermon? Then we shall be able to generalize and speak of good preaching in a continuous pastoral work. It will be impossible to escape glancing at some ideas already presented; but they rise to our view here, if they rise at all, in new and in quite necessary connections.

The first requisite to a good sermon is *that it be true*. We can get falsehood enough, without employing preachers to proclaim it. The devil rules the world by lies. A sermon should be like a man, with a body, soul, and spirit in it. The body of it ought to be truth. Nor is a sermon good simply because it is abstract truth. It must be religious truth, truth deriving its force and sanctions from the Bible. The ethical writers have provided for us an immense body of truth, and extremely important truth, which no wise preacher will disregard. But, as a preacher, he is to rest his plea on Divine revelation. Many forcible and conclusive arguments can be urged from the moralists against fraud and lying, for example. The Christian preacher starts almost where they leave off when he announces the eighth and ninth commandments in form, or in some of the many scriptures in which their substance is declared. Here is the commanding elevation on which a preacher stands above all other speakers to men. They rely for cogency and authority on the clearness or the beauty in which they can set their points, and the closeness with which they can bring them home to men. But a true preacher has no sooner made the people feel "thus saith the Lord," than he has secured authority and cogency. While a man says, "I think," his thought is to be measured by himself. It is as he is. When he declares, and with recognized truth, "the Lord says," men's minds are withdrawn from him; it is with the Lord they have to do. Gentlemen, you will sometimes feel your "presence weak and your speech contemptible," as you preach. The people will sometimes, perhaps, look at you, as if inquiring by what right you claimed their attention.

As soon as it is possible, get yourself out of view altogether, and let the truth of God come forth to shine in its own brightness. This disarms criticism, compels attention, and secures body to your sermon.

Settle it in your mind, that no sermon is worth much in which the Lord is not the principal speaker. There may be poetry, refinement, historic truth, moral truth, pathos, and all the charms of rhetoric; but all will be lost, for the purposes of preaching, if the word of the Lord is not the staple of the discourse; and the preacher will be little better than the wicked, of whom it is testified that "God is not in all their thoughts."

2. It must be *appropriate truth*, having the proper relation to the people who hear it, and to their circumstances. There are ancient heresies, for the refutation of which the Bible contains the materials, but it would be idle to labor on the setting forth of the refutation where no one is troubled, or likely to be, with the heresy. There are hard questions, like the tripartite nature of man, or the characteristics of Hades, on which the Bible has something to say, but their discussion before a village congregation of plain people would be useless. The circumstances of a

congregation may demand, and to a sympathetic mind would suggest, the right kind of theme. It is the Communion-Sabbath, for example. The sermon is a discussion of the law of tithes. It is an important law, and the sermon may be most true, but it is a right thing in the wrong place. The death of a pastor much beloved produces a deep feeling of solemnity among the bereaved people. How entirely an elaborate sermon on an important theme like the breadth of God's law may be thrown away, where a simple, earnest, affectionate word, from such a text as a minister desired to be laid on his bosom in his coffin, "Remember the word which I spake unto you," that his people might read it, or a plea for Him who died once and dieth no more, might reach all hearts. A nice instinct—the product of thought, sympathy, knowledge of human nature, and prayer—ought to guide in selecting the theme. If you have chosen well, your work is half done when you have read your text. Every one feels that you understand the situation, in some sense understand him. He is prepared to listen, and puts his mind in the attentive attitude: the fault will be yours if you lose your advantage. On the other hand, a remote and inappropriate topic vexes; produces a jar; is regarded as a kind of impertinence. You are rowing against the stream; your sermon will be in a great measure thrown away. When a man goes to a place on Saturday night and finds his sermon out of all relations to the people, he had better put it in his bag, shut himself up, and write out what, if he were in their place, he would feel suited him, and preach that. For all the purposes of a sermon, it will be more successful than his best effort that lies outside their horizon.

Here, I need not tell you, comes to the minister's aid his thorough acquaintance with his people. He feels with them. Their hearts throb, in a measure, against his bosom. He knows their needs, and, though his manner may be unpretending and his message simple and unadorned, it suits them, as cold water the thirsty.

The man who studies fitness above all else, will have great help given him in complying with rhetorical canons. He will be instructive. The people need to know something just then. They want to be told how they ought to think and feel. He tells them from the Word. In his eagerness to do this he is textually faithful. He desires to reflect its meaning. He is teaching from the Word. More than mere natural and legitimate curiosity influences them. They wish direction on a particular matter. He is bent on giving it. He is not drawn aside for the sake of some vivid bit of word-painting that could be brought in, or the presentation of some new and original speculation. He is not careful whether they count him intellectual or not. They need, and he has, ideas; and he gives them, on one matter. This secures *unity* in his discourse. But *fidelity* to the text, *instructiveness*, and *unity*, have always been placed in the forefront among the constituent elements of a good sermon.

3. It must be truth, *taught for the purposes of the truth.* God has revealed ideas for certain definite ends. A good preacher sets them forth for these ends. He proclaims that law which is holy, for the awakening of sinners and the guiding of the lives of believers. He lifts up Christ for the sake of attracting lost souls to the cross. This banishes subtle, treacherous, arrogant, proud, rebellious self. I have a good sermon, let me suppose, on the happiness of heaven. It pleases me, and mainly because it does, and is likely to make

a good impression in my favor, I preach it. Can I expect the blessing, as if I had reverently asked what these souls most needed among God's gifts, and had decided to show it to them, no matter what they thought of me?

This idea might be expressed in another way. Truth should be uttered *in a right spirit*. A man may set out the doom of the wicked in a tone of human threatening and bravado, as though he said, "This is what you will come to for disregarding *my* advice, and you well deserve it." This is enough to mar the truest sermon. A vitiating element goes with every sentence, when once the impression has been made that the preacher is vexed that men do not believe *him*. My brethren, remember two words spoken to masters (and the reason of them applies to you), "forbearing threatening, knowing that your Master also is in heaven." I know the sanctions of God's law are to be proclaimed. If any are silent regarding them, I am sorry for them and for their people. But I also know that the first place in which the terrors of the Lord are to make their impression is on the heart of the preacher, and that their true effect there is to make him not terrible, or terrific, but tender and persuasive. "Knowing, therefore, the terror of the Lord," the holiness of his law, the strictness of his justice, the ineradicable hatred with which he regards sin, the awfulness of being under his wrath, the fearfulness of falling as rebels into his hands—knowing these things from his word, "we persuade men." Let us remember, when we fling around with an unholy, brawling flippancy the awful denunciations of "tribulation and anguish," that we may be anticipating the sentence of those dearest to us, not to say our own. Let these truths be preached as fully as they are stated in the Bible, but with tenderness, with indescribable pity, with tears, such as Jesus shed over doomed Jerusalem.*

---

* A friend wrote me lately that he had heard the late Canon Kingsley preach in Westminster Abbey a sermon of peculiarly solemn and tender interest. My friend says:

"I do not know whether that was the last sermon ever he delivered, but it might well have been. Had he known it was almost the last message from heaven to man that he was to deliver I do not think he would have wished to change one word of it. His subject was Christ weeping over Jerusalem, and the particular passage, 'but ye would not,' the whole being a practical application of the ineffable love of God to man, and deliv-

4. *It should sustain the attention. Profit ends when weariness begins.* Not only so, but vexation with the preacher is apt to commence also. Now, attention is sustained by many forces in harmonious combination. If the *voice* be too low and indistinct the ear grows tired in catching the words. If it be occasionally loud and rough, the ear is offended, as is the eye with grotesque, awkward, or constrained action. If the words come too rapidly the sense is confused: if very slowly, like minute-guns at sea, the hearer grows impatient. A dull monotone is soporific: so is a continuous shout. There ought to be naturalness in the voice, and along with that periods of repose. Then there is room for emphasis, for expression, for variety of modulation. Otherwise Pope's lines

---

ered in the most simple, but tender and touching language I ever heard.

"We were only sorry when he concluded, although he preached a long sermon. He said that it might be the last time some of those there might hear his voice."

Who of us can tell when he is preaching his last sermon? Charles Kingsley, in earlier years, lacked the power that comes from clear, definite conviction as to the one way of life; but he had even then many of the elements that make a great man and a great preacher.

on commonplace versification are likely to be made good:

"If crystal streams ' with pleasing murmurs creep,'
The *hearer's* threatened—not in vain—with sleep."

But the *composition* may be monotonous, unbroken by incident, anecdote, or appeal, the cadences of sentences constructed on one model, rising and falling with a painful regularity. This should be guarded against. Vivacity of style is attainable, and applicable to any subject. He who spake in parables, who laid the birds, the lilies, the vines, the mustard-plant, the children under contribution for His discourses—*His* who "spake as never man spake"—surely sets an example to us as teachers. Language is singularly pliable, and its graces are appreciated even by the rude. The taste is not always correct. Indeed, taste itself is a variable element. Hervey's *Meditations among the Tombs* had, and still have, admirers. Jeremy Taylor, I know, has been extolled greatly, yet I have never felt the charm of his prose-poetry. Edward Irving has been regarded most favorably by many, yet his style has seemed to me stilted and affected. Yet I am sure, had I listened to any one of the three great men, I should have been made and kept attentive by the departure of the style from what is commonplace and indolent. I should have felt that each was trying to speak so that it would be agreeable to me to hear. So much we owe to our hearers. The effort is not incompatible with simplicity, force, and freedom from affection.

There should be *manliness* both in composition and delivery. Any trick obviously meant to startle; any attempt at stage-effect; any small device that might be proper enough in an after-dinner speech is felt to be unworthy the pulpit, and is condemned by good taste. Manliness implies straightforward simplicity, appreciation of the truths presented, and superiority to theatrical expedients. Many of the stories retailed in gossiping reports regarding eminent men are either colored or exaggerated; but there are well-authenticated accounts of great men descending to small shifts of ingenuity which you and I had better not imitate, and which even they could not have used often with success. For a certain gravity is expected, through a right human instinct, in ministers. Not that the particular attitude of the facial muscles is of any spiritual significance, one way or other; but men feel that while we are handling grave and most serious matters we ought to be serious. Did you ever see the pilot take a ship through a perilous passage? He is grave. I have seen the surgeon's knife drawn round the limb where an error of an inch would have been a terrible mistake. He was grave. I have heard a conscientious judge weigh and set out in the utmost fullness the evidence in a murder case, as earnestly bent on putting everything fairly as if his own life depended on the issue. Any levity here would be out of place; and, on the same principle, by the average of mankind, gravity will be looked for in us who deal with matters of life and death, and speak for God. That we have laughing muscles in the face is *prima facie* evidence that we are at liberty to laugh sometimes; but we have a great many muscles that have no special relation to preaching. All the power we gain by appeals to the risible faculties, we are likely to lose in other directions. Our attractiveness, then, had better depend on clearness of enunciation and style, on natural grace of expression, on manliness, force, and sufficient rapidity of movement, and on vehemence not out of proportion to the temper and tone of the matter we utter. The best preacher will be apt to suggest the language of the Psalm, "My heart was not within me, while I was musing the fire burned: then spake I with my tongue."

5. Good preaching should be *persuasive*. The motives, pleas, arguments, and appeals of the Bible should be presented in such a way as to lead men to move in the desired direction. Young preachers expect that reasons so cogent as they can state will command the assent and corresponding action of men. But, in point of fact, men are not thus uniformly moved. Men must be not only reasoned with, but convinced of your good will toward them. They have to be conciliated to unpalatable truth. The tone of the voice, the expression of face, the attitude of deference, or of imperious authority assumed toward them— all these have their influence. A remorseless logic, clear and irresistible by a logician, will be set at defiance by many a human heart that

would be influenced by a tone of tenderness in the voice, or a tear in the eye. Not that the tears are to supersede the argument, but to accompany it, and carry its force from the head to the heart. You may hear men preach where they seem to pierce, crush, and trample upon their opponents; and they make every hearer an opponent. Indignation, scorn, sarcasm, ridicule, all come into play; and the preacher, having it all his own way, treats himself to a triumph at the close. This is not persuasive. It lacks the first elements of true preaching. We should never assume hostility to us, or our views, on the part of our hearers. By their being in the house of God, and reverently and respectfully listening to us, His ministers, they give us the right to assume that they are not opponents but inquirers, not disputants but pupils. Let us treat them as learners, keep them as much as possible from the attitude of opposition, and carry them along without reminding them needlessly how much of their previous thinking we have beaten down.* Let us study

---

* The principle of this may be sometimes acted upon with advantage in intercourse with the members of a congregation.

His example who "reasoned in the Synagogue every Sabbath, and *persuaded the Jews and the Greeks.*" (Acts xviii. 4.)

How often has the method of that great master of pulpit eloquence, at Athens, been noticed and applauded. He begins with the facts lying around—the statues of the gods, the altars, the sacrifices. He even utters a word of commendation, of which our English version missed the point, making it " too superstitious." " I perceive that you are very religious." " Devout to excess" is Lewin's rendering of the word, δεισιδειμονεστέρους. They were proud of their religiousness.* Instead of being hurt by the allusion, they feel complimented. The men who politely said to him, "May we know what

---

Almost every community contains persons who are "nothing if not critical." Their importance lies in their peculiar ideas. They are delighted to give the new minister their "views." The young minister will be wise to evade the interview. Do not let these men commit themselves to their positions. Do not even hear, from them, their opinions. If you do, their self-love will set down half your teaching to the effort at refutation. Let them hear you, and possibly learn.

* See Lewin's *Life and Epistles of St. Paul,* Vol. I., p. 262 (note). This beautiful work throws much light on the apostle's journeys, and is worthy of careful examination.

this new doctrine, whereof thou speakest, is?" are not thrown off and repelled by any contemptuous allusion; nor is the attention fixed on any arguments but such as the hearers might be expected to appreciate and understand. "One of their own poets" is gracefully introduced, and the whole surroundings of a judicial court suggest to the speaker the impressive closing announcement of a final judgment, assured to all men by the raising of the Saviour from the dead. So when King Agrippa owns the force of Paul's appeal it is, "Almost thou persuadest me to be a Christian." So, gentlemen, in your preaching aim not only at showing abundance of "dry light;" let there be also the glow of affectionate interest that gives persuasive power. Let there be not body only, but also heart.

6. The sermon ought to be evangelical through and through, in body, soul and spirit. The word evangelical, in so far as it marks a party, I am sorry to employ. I use it here to mean full of the gospel of Jesus Christ. We are His messengers. What shall we do but deliver His message? It would be strange, indeed, if the thoughts and words and tone of the Master did not appear in what we His servants

say and do. We are to enlighten men. He is the light of life. We are to comfort men. He furnishes the comforts. We are to show men salvation. He is the Saviour. We are to strengthen men. He is their strength. We are to encourage men to holy obedience. He is the source of motive, of strength, of courage, and He is the perfect example. We are to guide men to the Father. He is the mediator. We are to show aliens how reconciliation is to be effected. He is the way. All out of Him are out of the way. He is the truth. To be out of Him is to be in deadly error. He is the life. To be out of Him is to continue " dead in trespasses and in sins." "No man cometh unto the Father but by Him." And when the Father would give men the light of the knowledge of His glory, how does He proceed? Why (2 Cor. iv. 6), He shines into their hearts. And how? To what does He turn men's gaze? Not to His mighty works; not to creative or providential wonders; not to geological or astronomical facts; not to the data on which Paley and Bell, and other admirable writers build up their argument from design; not to the still greater wonders of mind, but to " the face of Jesus Christ"—that face that was more marred that any man's; that endured the ruffian blows; down which the blood-drops trickled; that looked down on a mocking crowd from an ignominious cross. To that the Father points, as though He said, "Look at that spectacle—my Son, my holy, innocent Son, wounded for your transgressions, bruised for your iniquities. See in Him the holiness of my law, the rigor of my justice. See in Him the depth and tenderness of my love. Believe the love I have toward you, and give your hearts to me, in Him." This is God's method, my brethren. It is childish to inquire can we have any better? We have no choice about it. He gives you and me the gospel, of which Jesus is the sum, in His glorious person, His completed work, His effectual intercession, and He says to us, "Go preach the preaching that I bid thee." Let us go in His name and strength.

LECTURE VIII.

A LADY friend of mine tells me the following incident: A young lady, who was placed at the head of a house before she had become a good housekeeper, had to order dinner for her husband and herself. She had chickens for dinner the first day; the next a leg of mutton; and the third day, naturally desiring variety, she ordered the cook to have a leg of beef! So young preachers, not yet acquainted practically with their materials and the use they can make of them, feel the need of freshness and novelty, and sacrifice utility in the effort. I propose to devote this hour to the consideration of the best arrangement and distribution of our pulpit resources. If in anything my views seem to conflict with the ideas or the practices of other brethren, I need not say you will take them for what they are worth, and remember that it is by comparison of reasons and of experience that we reach conclusions of practical value.

(a) There is much *class-preaching*. "Young men," "the aged," "the young," are singled out, and formally addressed. The division is sometimes carried out very minutely, and I have known "young women," "the married," and "the single" specially addressed. "The working classes," are often so specified in Great Britain. A friend of mine heard a sermon in Ireland where the preacher descanted on the temptations to which men are liable. He divided them into the "temptations to the upper classes" and the "temptations to the lower classes." He always said "we" and "our" under the first head, never under the second.

I have some doubt of the wisdom of this course, though it cannot be denied that good and able men have effected much on such plans. But then they would have done good in any form of discussion of the truth into which they threw their thoughts; and it does not follow that this way is wise generally, because it has been made useful. When John the Baptist gave directions to publicans and soldiers, in classes, it was at their own request.

In the first place, the teaching of the Scripture is not formally distributed in this way. Every person has the strongest inducement to read the whole Bible. The whole field is digged by the sons of God, in the search for the treasure they want; and with the best results. Nor is the Scripture in any great degree a set of rules or rubrics, like the by-laws of a company, or the instructions to a ship's crew, but a set of great dominant principles, to be received into the heart, and to be intelligently applied to the affairs and exigencies of life. The application exercises and strengthens all the faculties. In the finding, digesting, and living out of truth, the whole man grows up in the likeness of Christ. The maiden does not find her chapter in the Bible from which she passes away when she comes among the mothers, to find her new section ready for her—but the whole Bible is the common heritage of mother and maiden.

There is danger of impairing habits of attention on this plan. When young men are being appealed to other classes in the audience will easily persuade themselves that they may be absent, or less attentive. It is desirable to keep all one's hearers alive to all that is being said. His special portion, let each man feel, may come in the next sentence. Let him be on the look-out for it. Give him no intimation that he is not concerned here, and may go mentally to repose.

Besides, the tendency is already great enough to hear—not for ourselves, but—for others. My observation is, that a sermon to young men in an ordinary church does not increase the attendance of that class in any noticeable degree, while there are preachers whose happiness it is to have a large, even a predominant, element of men—and there could be no greater happiness—in habitual attendance. It is a thoroughly inspiriting thing to see a mass of those to whom you can emphatically say, "Men and brethren!" I think we should aim at the men. Be manly, vigorous, courageous. Reason out of the Scriptures. Put the hearers' minds to work, and bring divine truth to bear on manly pursuits, and so clear off the aspersion that religion is for women and children. But while we are doing this with such effect as to bring the men, the women and children will not be missing.

It may seem as if some exception might be made in favor of preaching to children. But, as the years have gone on, I have modified my own views of that matter. I used to make sermons for the children specially, constructed and illustrated with regard to them; and it is quite true that the seniors usually gave good attention to them, and often heard with profit. But then the effect on the children is to be considered when your ordinary ministrations are proceeding. They had their portion. Now you are talking to the grown-up people. They may be excused from listening now. I think the wiser way is to throw in every day a bit of anecdote, or illustration that will suit the child-mind. Give no intimation that it is coming. But if you will say, "The children will see," or something of that nature, they are reminded that they are an integral portion of the congregation, and they get the habit of attending throughout. After the children get out of the nursery, I suppose in most families they get their meals at table with father and mother, hear the talk, and learn the ways of life. I think it is best for them to be similarly treated in the Church, and as a wise parent will do the carving and dividing so as to give the children what is fit for them, so a wise pastor will give to them their milk and their portion of meat, as they are able to bear it. When you become pastors, gentlemen, aim at bringing the children to

Church with the parents. They soon learn to "behave themselves in the House of God," and no stated service is all that it ought to be that is wholly and entirely without adaptation to them. It will be a sad abuse of a great blessing, if the Sabbath-school shall come to be regarded as the sufficient "Children's Church." Let us teach them to worship God with their fathers; let them be witnesses of baptisms and communions: they are part of the household.

(b) *Announced preaching* I do not regard with great favor. A man has, or his friends feel that he has, something out of the way to say, and he looks up a smart running title, and gives it out, or the newspaper does for him. You may see this in the New York newspapers any Saturday. I have never thought this a good plan, and would advise my brethren not to adopt it. It is regarded as a confession of general weakness. Your common things, it could hardly be supposed, would attract; but here is a sermon on "the iron that did swim," or the "little foxes," or Samson's foxes, or "Jehudi's penknife," and it is hoped the people will hear you thereon. And when there is no announcement, why, of course, the fair inference is, there is nothing peculiar; nothing worth hearing; nothing but the gospel!

Among the incidental evils of this announcing system, is the effect it has on the Christian community. There are enough of gypsies already, unattached hearers, who "go around" and hear the most "interesting" preachers. You get them the first time you are "announced," perhaps the second. But meantime your neighbor, or his deacons, will have taken note of the fact, and a rival announcement is in the field. You get out Goliath; he proclaims Samson. You intimate the Royal Dancing-Girl; and he forthwith produces the Witch of Endor, and the poor uninstructed owners of itching ears and vacant minds have a good time, and persuade themselves they are talking religion when discussing the relative merits of the performances. Let us leave all this to the Lyceum, the Lecturing Bureau, and the showmen. Let us be willing to go down as low as is needed to lift up sinners; but it is *we* that are to go down. This is to drag down the sacred desk, the office of the ministry, the Bible itself. Competitive rowing and running, and competitive oratory, may be well enough for the boys in school and college;

but competitive preaching is not among the elevating forces in the hand of the Church. And, as a rule, the least instructed hearers are those who have "heard everybody!"

(c) *Special preaching*, as a general rule, costs much and yields poor returns. By special preaching, I mean the sermons that are fitted to remarkable occasions—as the more formal Thanksgiving sermons, sermons on popular movements, and critical periods in the church's or the country's history. The interest in them is centered largely in the preacher's attitude to the subject. He is defining his position; he is maintaining his ground or his consistency; and the people have the pleasing satisfaction of sitting in judgment on him.

But, you say, should no notice be taken of the great events, the majestic steps of Jehovah's providence? I do not say that. I am for noticing them; and when you can get men like Chalmers and Robert Hall to descant on such events as the death of the Princess Charlotte, I am in favor of giving their efforts the widest publicity. But to ordinary men there is a better way. Two examples occur to me at this moment. The late Prince Albert, husband of Queen

Victoria, died on the Sabbath, and it was my duty to preach that evening. The subject for the evening was discussed in the usual way, and at some fitting time the event was alluded to with its lesson, and then prayer was offered for the newly-widowed Queen. It was one of the few cases I have witnessed where audible sobbing disturbed the preacher. Had a special sermon been made of it, the effect, I feel very sure, would have been less, and less salutary. The other occasion of which I think was the assassination of President Lincoln. I remember the spot where I heard it, and how it made my head swim. The very next service it was referred to, in some connection in the sermon, with marked effect, which no one could help noticing. Now, suppose in these cases the expectation of the people raised by the announcement of a special sermon, every lawyer, every man that ever made a speech, every man almost, has a double train of thought in his mind — that which the event itself suggests to him, and that which relates to your treatment of the theme. "He has a great, stirring topic; he has announced it; he has taken time for special preparation; now let us see is he equal to the occasion." This is an unfavorable condition of mind for receiving spiritual impression; and you keep your hearers out of it by avoiding the "special" element.

I am inclined to put among the "specials" a great proportion of the funeral addresses. Now and then an outstanding and prominent Christian challenges notice, and is felt by common consent to deserve it in the pulpit. But, as a general rule, you will find funeral sermons the hardest, and the least productive of good, among your efforts. A tender-hearted man is eager to speak responsively to the warm feelings of bereaved and mourning relatives to whom the deceased has been so much, and who, in their fresh grief, think only of his virtues. But he cannot, ordinarily, speak as strongly as they feel; and in the effort he may speak with an emphasis, the foundation of which is not recognized by the rest of his audience. The general hearer, to whom the deceased is described in the strongest terms that delineate saintship, will measure your language next Sabbath-day by the application of it which he witnessed, and will conclude that exalted Christian character is of easier attainment than he had understood; for our hearers often know the departed better than we do. The obituary notices in the Scripture are commonly brief, and those of the pulpit are commonly too long. You will do wisely to begin and go through this most difficult and delicate part of your ministerial labor with a moderate and measured use of language; nor will you lose by this in the end. The judgment and conscience of the Christian people will be with you; and you will commonly find the ripest and most cultivated Christians anxious beforehand that the least possible personal description of them should be given at their funerals.

Now, you may suppose that the elimination of these "occasional efforts" will leave little but the dead level monotony of the regular sermon, as much like its predecessor and its successor as one hymn-book is like another. This, however, is by no means the case. In lieu of the foregoing expedients for keeping up interest, let there be *vigorous consecutive teaching*. For this provision may be made in various ways. One is by sequence of thought. Christ, as the mediator, has been, let us say, your theme on one Lord's Day. His functions as Priest, as Prophet, as King, may follow in succession. Or in connection with any one of these you branch off into the collateral truth, of the lack in man that necessitates the office, and how it is supplied. From the kingly office of Christ you may pass to the forms of obedience we render, the immunities we enjoy, the prospects before us. Care is taken to say, "Last Lord's Day we saw, etc. To-day, we follow it up by considering," etc. The hearers gradually get the notion that you have a plan; that you are aiming at instructing them; and commonly their minds will meet you half way. Good is done when you dispossess them of the idea that you go to the traditional sermon-store and take out whatever comes easiest to hand. Or there may be formal sequence, as when you intimate a course of sermons. Once a year a minister might, with great advantage, have such a course. The Lord's Prayer, the Ten Commandments, the Miracles of our Lord, the Parables, the Epistles to the Churches, furnish materials for such continuous and connected addresses. Biography, history, the beatitudes, the arguments of the Epistles, may make the subjects of such instruction. The minor prophets, each of them furnishing material for a sermon in which you popularize what is commonly called "introduction," furnish a most useful line of instruction. Take the average

young person in our congregation and bid him find
Amos. He is mentally paralyzed for a moment. It
takes him a little time to collect his scattered faculties
to the unfamiliar task. Then begins a nervous
turning of handfuls of leaves, with a concurrent
mental effort to run over the list of the prophets in his
mind, so as, if possible, to locate Amos. And all this
is typical of his mental state regarding the contents
of Amos. There is to many a sort of Sahara in the
middle of their Bibles which they should be made to
explore. Genesis they know, and something about
Moses, and David, and Goliath; and the New Testament they know; but Hosea, and Zephaniah, and
Ezekiel, who are these? Gentlemen, at the risk of
seeming to repeat a cuckoo-song, let me declare again
and again, that what is most wanted among professing Christians is knowledge of their Bibles.
Christians know too little of it; skeptics know but
little of it, and great masses of the otherwise intelligent but ungodly of our population do not know it at
all. Ignorance of it is the soil in which the rank
growths of "isms" of every kind flourish. Nor is
this ignorance only among the rude peasantry from
foreign lands, such as are transported across the con-

tinent to be drawers of water for Mormonism. It is surprising to every man who has looked into it, how many native-born Americans from Maine, New Hampshire, Vermont, Massachusetts, and New York, shrewd, well-informed, posted in all newspaper themes, are yet lamentably ignorant of the letter of their Bibles. It is essential to the growth of piety and virtue to change all this. Never mind whether you are thought learned, eloquent, strong, or accomplished. You shall not have lived in vain if it can be written over your grave, "He made the people understand the Scriptures."

It is not needful to remind you of the two quite distinct methods of pursuing knowledge which have been employed by men. In the one the inquirer forms a theory, and then looks around for the facts to fit into it. This plan charmed the daring, brilliant, Oriental mind. On the other he collects his facts, and enough of them, and builds up his theory on them. Practical Rome was more inclined to this method. With the introduction of Christianity, the human mind received a mighty impetus, and, as we see in the vigorous preaching of Augustine, turned to the way of dealing with the data, and founding on them the

THE FACTS AND THE TEXTS. 191

theory. With the growth of superstition, the Aristotelian method was resumed, and we get to the elaborate trifling of the Schoolmen, whose theology resembled, in subtlety and in want of foundation, the Greek philosophy. The Reformation broke up these card-board castles that men had constructed, and sent men after the fashion of Augustine to the great mass of data in the Scriptures. Bacon's inductive method set men to the study of nature. The result is apparent in the material advances of modern times. Three hundred years of inductive philosophy have done more to enable men to rule over and subdue the earth than a thousand preceding years

"Through all their creeping dark duration."

Now we want this Baconian method applied to the Bible-study. What facts are in nature, as in gases, in minerals, in atoms, to the student of matter, Bible texts are to the theologian. These we sift, examine, analyze, classify. Instead of evolving conceptions and theories from our own brain—like the crystalline spheres with which Ptolemy filled the heavens— brilliant and baseless—and proving them by our conceptions of the fitness of things, we build tnem up on the well-ascertained data of revelation. They are no stronger than their foundation. If we have reasoned rightly they are as strong. As the measure of the power of a chain or a machine is the strength of its weakest point, so our theories and conclusions are no stronger than our weakest reasonings regarding the revealed truths. But working on this plan with the modesty of true science, intensified because we are dealing with the declarations of the living God, we go from strength to strength, every conquest we make being assured, and every trophy we take having inscribed on it, "Not unto us, O Lord, not unto us, but unto Thy name be the glory." Nor can you fail to see that this plan honors God the speaker, as true philosophy honors God the worker. Here are facts that do not fit into my philosophy. Then the philosophy must give way to the facts. We must keep our system open, so to speak, till a place is found for the facts. Here in religious thought are truths and texts that do not fit into my system. Then my system must give way to them. It does not support the texts; the texts must support it. If they do not, it goes down, and it ought to go down.

For man is not a creator, but an observer; not even so much an inventor as a discoverer. He does not, in his best philosophy, set out with a daring guess as to centric and concentric circles in the heavens. He begins with the falling apple, the sparkling dewdrop, the shining candle on the earth. He works upward to stars and suns. The task is slow, unambitious, and toilsome, but the reward is sure. Now true theology is the counterpart of that acquisition, the written word of God corresponding to the glorious works of God. We toil among texts and words, instead of starting from without and above, with a comprehensive philosophy evolved from our own consciousness. Our path is lowly, and at first obscure, but it shineth more and more unto the perfect day.

Our friends of the Episcopal Church have retained from pre-Reformation times the "Church Year," with its Christmas and Easter, and other holy times connected in the thought of the Church with the events of the Church's founding. The good and the strength derived in this way are not unmixed, but a certain variety of theme is secured. They have not, indeed, in England, retained any firmer hold on the people thereby. Take the southern portion of Great

Britain, in which this system with all the prestige and influence of an establishment was set forth, and after a couple of centuries there is not an established Church in Christendom with so many pronounced dissenters from it as the English. And when men leave it, they leave the bishop, the prayer-book, and the Christian year behind absolutely. No dissenting community has attempted to reproduce them. Take Scotland, on the other hand, with no such arrangements, with a poor establishment, frowned on habitually by power, and without prestige. It, too, has had dissenters from its pale, numerous and earnest. But when they have gone, it has not been in protest against the Church institutions, but for them. They have gone in an effort to keep them pure. None of them renounce Presbytery, their Confession, or their Catechism. Every "body" sets up its own Presbytery, instates in authority the Confession and the Catechism. All this I mention to show that a very exaggerated idea may be entertained of the power to interest and retain of the festivals and anniversaries of that "Church Year," around which Keble wove the chaplets of a very attractive Christian poesy. But in another way we may attain all the variety we need, and without any element of weakness. We can call out and promote a true church-life, on the line of our New Testament institutions. When the ordinance of baptism is administered, let all the truth therewith connected be brought before the people regularly, patiently, diligently. When the young become communicants, let the nature of a Christian profession be explained and the duty enforced; and so we realize all the benefits without any of the weakness of " confirmation." When the Lord's Supper is observed—and it ought probably to be more frequent than it is—all the mystery and charm of incarnation, all the majesty of law met by substitution, the one for the many and the innocent for the guilty, and all the pleading pathos of the crucifixion, may pass under review, appealing at once to judgment, conscience, memory, and affections. This may seem to you a kind of truism, a thing so obviously right that no need exists to enforce it. You are mistaken here. The Lord's Supper is sometimes observed with very little reference to it in sermon or prayers, little foregoing instruction, little subsequent helps to recall obligation and strive after consistency.

So, when the choice and ordination of an officer becomes the duty of the Church, should we have the exposition of popular rights and responsibilities, and the divine, scriptural warrant for ordination. The Church's nature, and the Church's functions as a living organism of which Jesus Christ is the head and the Holy Ghost is the heart, come under notice, and the church-life is maintained concurrently with the life of the individual soul.

If it be said that this course fosters undue and excessive thought regarding the Church, and brings men into that undesirable temper known as sectarianism or bigotry, the reply is at hand. An intelligent acquaintance with the principles underlying church-life is not the soil in which bigotry flourishes. It is the ignorant who are sectarian. It is one thing to understand what we mean in baptizing, ordaining, and commemorating the Saviour's love; it is quite another, ignorantly and arrogantly, to despise those who think differently. As a general rule, the most practically catholic Christians are those who have the most intelligent acquaintance with their Church principles, and the most enlightened attachment thereto; even as the best and most devoted husbands and fathers are commonly the best neighbors and the most public-spirited citizens.

The Church of Christ is to be aggressive in the world. Her activities find scope in missionary labor at home and abroad. But a Christian community will not perform its functions in this respect without instruction, motive, and direction. It is no mean part of a Church's life to learn and do God's will in this department, and the minister can usually find few topics more fitted to instruct and animate his charge than missionary work furnishes. Let the day on which foreign missions receive the people's gifts be marked by a vigorous presentation of the condition of heathenism, its unconscious fulfillment of prophecy, its illustration of Scripture truth, its utter helplessness without the Gospel, and its exhibition of what we would be in the like condition. When home missions have their day, let the moral and spiritual condition of the country pass under review. Let there be turned on it the light of God's word; let its dark places be exhibited; let our national weaknesses and sins be remorselessly laid bare; let the actual condition of the Churches and the masses be faithfully portrayed; let the obligations of the Christian people be enforced; let the truths which formed the foundation of the Christian Church, and again of this Republic, be emphasized, and a genuine public spirit will be fostered, such as makes men Christian patriots. The novelty and the first flush of missionary excitement have passed; the mere romance of the enterprise is gone. The work is now to rely for prosecution on calm, intelligent, reflecting Christian principle. Knowledge has to supply motive. A race has grown up that knows not Brainerd, and Judson, and Carey, and Boardman, and Goodell, and Moffat. The abundance of general literature crowds out the missionary. People will not long give sympathy, prayer, and money to that of which they have no knowledge; and in our time a Church that has not missionary zeal, is like a body paralyzed on one side. It is incapable of taking exercise, and the debility increases.

The poor among us, again, constitute a means of developing a true Church-life. Our Protestant system, by its very success in fostering a manly, vigorous, self-reliant spirit, has thrown us out of sympathy, in some degree, with patient, zealous, enlightened effort for the poor. When there is an unusual pressure on the indigent we make a generous contribution. When we have done that, we are apt to think we have done all. But it is not so. Surely there is a *via media* somewhere between the mediævalism which divided society into the two distinct and well-marked classes—the givers, who meant well, and the receivers, who fared ill by sinking into needy and greedy dependence—the "religious," who dispensed, and the ignorant and degraded who lived on, alms—between this and the Protestant method, which remits the whole question of the general poor to the civil authorities. Surely the Church may yet fall on the plan of those earlier self-denying laborers whose virtues and successes gave prestige to the monastic system, who taught and elevated while they helped materially, who lifted up mind and soul while feeding and clothing the body. To instruct the large class not inside our Churches, to bind them by the gentle bonds of love to the Church's institutions, to educate them out of jealousy and suspicion of the rich, and into self-helpfulness, forethought, and all prudent thrift and self-respect, is surely a work worthy of the American Church in the nineteenth century. There is no want of benevolence in the American people. But it is benevolence that is unintelligent, that is credulous, that is impulsive, and, moreover, that will not take trouble. If ever the problem of pauperism is to be solved, Christian love must take it in hand. Law can only, like the surgeon's knife, cut off what is hopelessly gone, or mortifying. Force can only restrain; it has no reforming capacity. Police can only stand between our houses and lives and the human beasts of prey, that grow up in our social wilderness; it cannot tame them. Christian love, catching its inspiration from the cross and drawing its power from Him who hung upon it, alone can appreciate the situation, catch the eye, win the confidence, and gain the heart of the criminal and reckless, who are constantly passing out of the ranks of neglected pauperism. Given, a Church that has lost positive faith, that is letting the doctrines go one by one, to which God is mere infinite good nature, the Cross a mere legend and the Holy Ghost a figure of speech, and I know no better restorative than to have it brought in good earnest to deal with souls dead and utterly perishing in their own corruption. The "fall" will become real, depravity real, need of regeneration real, the blood of Jesus real, the wages of sin real, the gift of God real, as the abortive effort is made by kindly platitudes to call out spiritual life. Human wickedness mocks all superficial dealing with symptoms, and compels us to come back to the radical truth of revelation, "If any man be in Christ, he is a new creature," and in no other way—"old things are passed away; behold all things are become new." * A lazy, indolent church tends toward unbelief. An earnest, busy church, in hand-to-hand conflict with sin and misery, grows stronger in faith.

One thing more only, gentlemen, shall I add: In your ministry, and in all systematic church-work, try to magnify the family. We have dwelt on individual responsibility, power, and capacity, until the individual has appeared to be the exclusive unit of society.† The Lord makes much of the family, binds together parent and child, and so generation and

---

* 2 Cor. v. 17.

† A truth neglected avenges itself by leaving space for an opposite error. A half truth told perpetually has a corresponding Nemesis in its train. We have cried up the individual. But, behold! here is a good half of the individuals of the race to whom we deny equal rights and privileges. Hence the crying and screaming one hears from the aggrieved claimants. But a cry or a scream out of a crowd is evidence, as

generation. His offer of mercy runs thus, "Believe on the Lord Jesus Christ, and thou shalt be saved, and thy house." Work on this principle with your charges. A strong Church is made up of well-ordered families, where intelligent, Christian parents bring up their children in the fear of the Lord, where the home of the week has its counterpart in the home of the Sabbath, where the hopes and joys of the living, and the blessed memories of the dead, bind to the Lord and his Church, where young men and maidens are glad when it is said unto them, "Let us go up unto the house of the Lord," where the tranquillity, and purity, and holy peace, the light and the love, form to the opening minds of children a type and prophecy of the eternal Sabbath, and the heaven above.

---

has often been said, that some one is being hurt in the pressure. The candid and just course is, not to cry it down, but to look and inquire, and relieve the pressure where it hurts. Instead of pooh-poohing "women's rights," will it not be wiser and better to return to the divine method of honoring the family, guarding its rights, defining its relations, and the duties due to it. If it be said many women are unmarried, the reply is that marriage is not necessary to a family. There are in the United States many well-ordered and happy families of the unmarried—homes like that of Bethany, with Lazarus, and Martha, and Mary, his sisters, in which there does not seem to have been any married person.

LECTURE IX.

THE PREACHING REQUIRED BY THE TIMES.

It may be readily admitted that the truth had to be presented in one form in the apostolic times, in another in the days of the Reformation, and in yet another in our own era. Heathenism and corrupt Judaism had to be dealt with by the apostles, corrupt Christianity by the reformers, unbelief and various forms of worldliness by us. But in all these cases the truth is the same, though its opponents are different. It was with the weapons of Paul, Peter, and John the battle of the Reformation was fought and won. It is from this same armory we are to equip ourselves for the conflicts of our day. The methods of employing the truth must needs vary in some degree with the varying forms of ungodliness; but "the truth" is a fixed quantity. Its nature and the history of human thought all go to show what might be presumed from its origin—that it is capable of adaptation to all the emergencies of human thought and life.

But, in actual fact, "times" are less variable for the purposes of a preacher than is commonly supposed. Steamships and railway-cars differ materially from the conveyances they have superseded, but their passengers have, as men and women, undergone no corresponding change. Human nature, in its essential elements, has been the subject of no substantial alteration. The carnal mind is still enmity against God. Man is still so ignorant that he needs a great Prophet; so guilty that he needs atonement; so rebellious that he needs to be conquered for the Lord; so helpless that he needs to be defended; so wayward that he needs to be "established" and kept by the mighty power of God.

Nor does the enemy of our souls discover or invent a great deal. Satan is a finite being. He has not materially modified or improved his devices since the beginning. The Babylon of the Apocalypse retains all the essential lineaments of the ancient Babylon.*

---

* See the *Two Babylons, or Nimrod and the Papacy*, by the Rev. A. Hislop, a most ingenious and interesting work.

Worldliness in our time is, in substance, the same as before the Flood. There was complete absorption in the material interests and social affairs of the present life, to the exclusion of God and the future. " They did eat, they drank, they married wives, they were given in marriage ; " " they bought, they sold, they planted, they builded " in Sodom much as they do in our cities and towns.* If you study the history of our first parents' temptation you will see how few improvements the tempter has effected in all these thousands of years. He is still standing by the tree of knowledge; still telling women and men that they shall be as gods, knowing good and evil; still insinuating doubts concerning divine attributes; still saying: " You may be guided by me, and disregard God, and ye shall not die." Study the temptation of our blessed Lord, and you will see that the policy tried in vain on him is still the diabolical policy applied to man. To sow the seeds of distrust of God, and confidence in self; to

---

* Luke xvii. 27, 28. The danger to very many men, now as then, is in things lawful in themselves. They engross and preoccupy, and men know not till the end comes, and they are carried away.

point out easy roads to elevation on Satan's plan; or to lead men into self-destroying presumption—this is, even now as then, the aim of Satan in all the agencies he establishes and in all the movements he inspires.

The tendency with each generation is to think its own time the strangest and most peculiar the world ever saw. How many patients in the hospitals imagine their cases unique and unprecedented! How many persons suppose their lives without parallel in human experience! When I have been speaking in various cities and towns in the interests of temperance, I have been told in at least fifty cases: "This is the very worst town for intemperance in the whole country." My informants simply knew it better than they did any other. So we, because we know our own times better than others, are apt to think them unlike any others. There is, perhaps, even a spice of self-love in this delusion. Like criminals, or like the poor sufferers under the surgeon's knife, we are flattered by the idea that our circumstances are not ordinary and commonplace. But, as to all the great facts of human life and the underlying principles of human conduct, "the thing that hath been is that which shall be, and that which is done is that which shall be done; and there is no new thing under the sun." * This statement, if it be just, tends to show that if we know thoroughly, and tell clearly the truth, it will suit our times, and all times, as truly as the unchanged sunlight suits all human eyes and the pure atmosphere all healthy lungs from the beginning.

Yet these considerations do not preclude our studying the features of our times and the best methods of offering and urging the blessings of the covenant of grace. But it is noticeable that in many studies on this subject the bad elements of our era only, or mainly, are presented, and the preacher is placed in antagonism to all the great forces at work in society. This is very discouraging, but is it necessary? Are there not good tendencies as well as bad of which the preacher may take note? Is not the Lord Jesus, from his "glorious high throne," subsidizing many human movements and yoking them to the chariot of the everlasting Gospel? It would be ungrateful in spirit and it

---

* Eccl. i. 9.

would be unwise in policy to ignore these. Therefore I propose to indicate to you some of the tendencies of our time—good no less than evil—to which we should have an intelligent regard in making our selection of topics, and in determining the tone and treatment they demand.

There are evils so salient that we must take account of them, and yet without supposing that our cotemporaries are sinners beyond all that went before them. Intelligence is now collected from all quarters. It is rendered picturesque and striking. The crimes and casualties of the world are served up with our breakfasts. We may suppose the world getting worse when it is only getting better known. So we may be tempted, like the paganism of Greece and Rome, to put the Golden Age in the past, while Christianity places it in the future. Paganism had the traditions and broken memories of Eden. It had not the prophecy of the reign of righteousness. It had the knowledge of its own corruptions, and it had no vision of the kingdom of grace and holiness.

1. Among the noticeable evils of our day is the overestimate of riches as a means of happiness and

proof of success in life. In the Old Testament, where, in the absence of completed written revelation, Divine Providence expressed divine regard in material prosperity, "wealth and riches" are magnified,* not, indeed, without many a pungent word as to their insufficiency, transiency, and deceptiveness.† We retain much of the Old Testament view of them, and of a very little religion in a rich man we are apt to think it "a great deal for him." The conquests over nature have been signal and many. The earth has yielded up her stores to trained laborers. Gold has come in rich abundancy in our time, and men are dazzled by its brilliancy. Commerce has been eager, enterprising, and successful. Money has been acquired with unwonted rapidity by numbers, and the publicity given to all such "successes" in our life magnifies their number and greatness, and stimulates the ambitious. This fact determines the duty of the preacher. What was made incumbent on Timothy we are not to evade. "Charge them that are rich in this world that they be not high-minded, nor trust in uncertain riches, but in the living God,

---

* 2 Chron. i. 12 ; Ps. cxii. 3.
† Job xxi. 13 ; Prov. xiii. 11, 22 ; Ps. xlix. 6.

who giveth us all things richly to enjoy." * Perhaps because we have not titles, distinctions, and hereditary honors, and are to so great a degree a commercial community, there is a tendency among us to pay court to wealth, from which even the Church is not exempt, which is at once inconsistent with our republican and with Christian simplicity. There is a vulgar, jealous envy of the rich which makes men ready to believe the worst things of them—a base passion on which communism and all kindred "isms" live, with which the Bible has no sympathy; but, on the contrary, it urges—and so must we—that the rich make to themselves friends of the Mammon of unrighteousness, that when they fail they may receive them into everlasting habitations.† The

---

* 1 Tim. vi. 17-19.

† Luke xvi. 9. In natural recoil from "indulgences" and salvation by money, Protestants have been shy of this text. Why should they be? Our Lord, naturally taking the language from the foregoing parable, counsels men to employ what in the steward's hand was unrighteous Mammon in doing good to those who need it (assumed to be God's children), that when it failed them (apparently the true reading) by its departure, or by theirs, these friends should welcome them into everlasting habitations. This is very different indeed from a salvation by "money and price."

whole subject of Christian obligations regarding money, of systematic consecration, of maintenance of God's ordinances, receives less attention now than in apostolic times, partly because ministers shrink from seeming to plead their own cause. Few of them have preached as much as the Apostle Paul alone wrote on this eminently practical topic. Nor is it only on the positive side that we are to teach believers how to use their gifts. There are real perils to all—to the young especially—in the eager race for riches, of which the pulpit ought to give unmistakable warning. For every man who goes to moral ruin through narrow means there are two who stumble over fortunes and go to destruction, or who, in the mad pursuit of them, "fall into temptation and a snare, and into many foolish and hurtful lusts, which drown men in destruction and perdition."

2. The extravagant and selfish use of money is a trouble of our times. It is not merely that men lay out much money; if the objects be legitimate they have a right to expend their own. The sin and contemptible folly lie in laying it out for the purpose of being able to proclaim the lavish expenditure. The

luxury of heathen Rome in her decay is being reproduced. When Apicius offered wine with pearls dissolved in it; when Lollia Paulina's second-best dress cost one hundred and fifty thousand dollars; and when Roman society applauded and envied, the rottenness had already superseded the brave simplicity of early and ever-victorious Rome. The iron was becoming mixed with the clay. Our danger looms up in this direction. Vulgar, ostentatious, objectless expenditure does not strike us as it ought. We begin to "live delicately" like Tyre and ancient Babylon; we ought to be afraid of inglorious decadence like theirs.

If there is to be any effective protest against all this the Church should surely raise it. If any light is cast on it in the Scriptures, the pulpit ought to reflect it. Christian women ought to set an example of modesty, self-restraint, and womanly dignity, to the community. So long as distinction comes by dress and decoration, and the joys of life consist, in any marked degree, in the display of fashionable costume and costly jewelry, so long will the temptation be irresistible to the weaker part of the sex to procure these essentials at any cost, even the sacrifice of all that true woman cherishes. "She that liveth in pleasure is dead while she liveth"* is plain and practical truth which the pulpit should re-echo. Where is the use of setting up Magdalen Asylums on the one hand, and on the other, opening up the slippery paths on which he feet of "careless daughters" stumble, so that they become qualified by sin and misery to be the objects of such "charity?" Why should panics, losses, and mortifying collapses be necessary to recall man to the truth of things, the uses of money, and the objects of life? There is no want of clear speaking on these subjects in the Word. It is bold, courageous, searching. It strips off conventional disguises, exposes all sophistry of selfishness, and magnifies manly, womanly superiority to childish display and ostentatious trappings. It makes no more of royal purple, and glittering gems on the godless, than we do of the feathers and war-paint of the savage. As the Redeemer was not carried away, like His disciples, with admiration of the goodly stones with which Jerusalem's temple was built, for His eyes had seen the heavenly Zion, so the soul that has been taught the

---

* 1 Tim. v. 6.

value of unsearchable riches, and the glory of the inheritance of the saints, rates at their true worth the transient dignities that money or position confers. To form the judgment and correct human estimates is no mean part of the work of the ministry. Present possessions are to be seen and rated in the light of the enduring and eternal.

3. Our time overestimates the value of physical studies. They do, undoubtedly, interest, fascinate, and in some degree, refine. Nor is their attraction wholly sentimental. They enrich and multiply power. Applied chemistry, electricity, and mineralogy render substantial service to mankind, while they open up the way to wealth to the possessors of the power of knowledge. Men who disclose the secrets of nature, like the wise men and magicians of the Orient, secure the favor of princes and the confidence and veneration of the masses. Hence, like the wise men of old, they become recognized as authorities on all subjects. Yet it does not follow that a man whose natural powers and close observation have made him an authority on rocks, minerals, or magnetism, should be, therefore, an oracle in morals or religion. A microscope does not magnify an obscure point in

law or casuistry. A telescope does not bring spiritual forces any nearer, or disclose Him who is invisible. Yet is this forgotten, and an eminent specialist in natural history will be presumed by many infallible in philosophy or religion.

The pulpit has a duty here, not to frown on or discourage physical science, which has a distinct and most honorable sphere, but to show its place, and to constrain the attention of the physicist himself, if he will hear, to the great concurrent facts of the moral and spiritual world. It is not science that does harm; but its exclusive study. The mind molded by the methods of this study grows insolent and arrogant, suspects and rejects the facts that cannot be verified under the dissecter's knife or in the crucible. Nor is it true and thorough science, as a rule, that is skeptical, but half-educated and short-sighted technical knowledge, which only takes cognizance of what it has scrutinized—like the blind man who felt the leg of an elephant and pronounced the animal to be an upright pillar, while his blind companion, who got hold of the trunk, pronounced him soft and flexible like a serpent.

The teaching of divine truth, not controversially,

but clearly and positively, is the check on their excesses. Natural philosophers study God as Creator. Christian ministers have to exhibit Him also as Father. The natural philosopher has one record, the Christian minister has two. The natural philosopher is apt to make law inviolable; to sell the universe to law. The Christian minister sees God in the laws, and counts them but his thoughts. A boy has a repeater given him, but does not know it from an ordinary watch. He hears its tickings and watches its hands. He knows the laws of its nature, he supposes. But when he is shown its repeating power and hears it strike, he is amazed, startled. But he soon sees that its repeating power is as much the law of the watch as its time-keeping power, and was as truly provided for in its structure. Natural philosophy, at the present moment, is sorely puzzled by prayer. It is an impenetrable mystery to it. It reasons against it as the sophist did against walking. What shall we do? As the philosopher did, in reply, who walked, so "let us pray." However otherwise mistaken, he had a good, true thought, who said:—

"Brothers! spare reasoning; men have settled long
That ye are out of date, and they are wise;

Use their own weapons; let your words be strong,
  Your cry be loud, till each scared boaster flies;
Thus the Apostles tamed the pagan breast,
They argued not, but preached; and conscience did the rest." *

We should hardly think of making an overestimate of the fine arts a special mark of our time. It is the common snare of all wealthy and luxurious communities to overrate the imitative products of men. How high art-culture may be, and how low the moral and spiritual life of its votaries may be, one may see in the Medicis, in Leo X., and his time, in the Augustan age of Rome, and of France. Corrupt religious systems easily accommodate themselves to such tastes, and embody their results in worship; but there is no evidence of resulting spiritual gain. The tribute to art has commonly been paid at the expense of religion.

Nor do we specify, though we do not ignore, the tendency to idolize genius. To how many has Charles Dickens been a prophet? But men are not necessarily authorities in all fields because they are effective painters or word-painters. As absurd as

---

* VERSES ON VARIOUS OCCASIONS, by John H. Newman. (This was written in 1833.)

to make a pedestrian, whose feats of so many miles in so many hours have amazed or amused, an authority on Christian walk and conversation, or to rely on a man for astronomical wisdom because he was tall and had good eye-sight, or on Turner as a botanist because he painted stone-pines, or as a ship-builder because he succeeded on ships—as absurd is it to clothe a man with authority in every department of human thought because he is eminent in one. The truth with which we have to do has its own plane, its own appropriate evidences, its own tests, its own authorities, and the wayfaring man, though a fool, is as open to the spirit's guidance in it as is the most penetrating genius. "Let God be true, and every man a liar."

Turn now to the cheerful aspects of our times, and in view of which Christian preachers ought to be strong and of a good courage.

1. We hail as a good sign the independence of thought of our time. Human authority does not go unchallenged. The mere name of Aristotle or of Plato does not silence an objector. The old kings of mind, who ruled so long and so despotically, "have gone out of business." Men do not bow their heads at the

name of the Fathers. Councils are regarded as gatherings of so many fallible men, and no nearer infallibility from their meeting than a thousand ciphers without a whole number are nearer to value from the addition of another thousand. "The Church" does not, by the mere mention of the name, forbid inquiry. The State is limited in its functions. Time was, and yet is, where to decline its clergy must be constructive disloyalty to its king. Men feel their right to discuss, examine, and investigate. They are like children new-fangled with the pretty things physical science has brought them; but the childhood will pass away. If some are in the state of mind described by Lord Bacon,* "a little philosophy inclineth a man's mind to atheism," others are at the further and happier stage, "but depth in philosophy bringeth men's minds about to religion."

The Christian minister need not fear this independence. Let us rejoice in it. We stand on a revelation that says, "Prove all things, hold fast that which is good."† It is a good time in which to live. These gales will do no permanent harm. If branches

---

* Bacon's Essays, xvi., on Atheism. † 1 Thess. v. 1.

and trunks come down, it is mostly the rotten, and the growing and healthy trees grow better and take root the deeper for the blasts. Any thought is better than none; a breeze with even wild waves is healthier than a stagnant, dead sea. We have, I do believe, greatly overrated the relative power of infidelity in our time. When Bishop Butler issued his Analogy he stated in the preface that it had come to be taken for granted that the Christian religion was not worth arguing about, and men were hastening to take revenge for the restraints it had imposed on them. Where is there any infidelity now with the genius, the boldness, the conscious power, the popular acceptance it enjoyed in the days of Rousseau, Voltaire, and Diderot? There is more living religion in the Episcopal Church, or in any one of two or three English denominations now, than in all Great Britain in the beginning of this century. There never was as strong and intelligent a Christian sentiment in the world as there is at this moment, never so rich a Christian literature, never were so many living believers. There is more Christian knowledge in Europe than at any time for the last thousand years, and America and Australia represent a new world of life and vigor. Nor is the heart of Christendom less hopeful than it ever was. "The ages of faith" of which many rhapsodize, were ages of much superstition, of crusades, of Flagellantes, of intolerance, of schoolmen, of Guelphs and Ghibellines, of much baptized heathenism. The Church of Jesus Christ fears nothing from real free thought. Her members are its truest friends and wisest patrons. She does not tremble before Greek as bringing in all heresies. Her travelers explore the lands of the Bible, dig into the ruins of empires, exhume the bones of ancient kings, and feel assured that the alleged home of the Bible will not disown it. History is not dreaded; criticism of the destructive kind, as it was called, has had its day. The friends of the Bible do not "peep and mutter," but stand on the housetops and call for evidence from every quarter. Ancient MSS. are worth their weight in gold to Christians; mummies from Nineveh, and bricks from Babylon—all are in demand; and Christian scholarship counts on their corroboration of the Christian faith. It is a grand time in which to live and labor as ministers. Our preaching should respond to every cry for light and life. We proclaim liberty to the captives. We have no wish to command the winds of free thought back to their cave. Christianity emancipates mind, and brings it into discipleship to Him whose service is freedom. It welcomes all restlessness under human yokes, and says to every human spirit that is tugging at its chains, "If the Son shall make you free ye shall be free indeed."*

2. There is more humanity in this age than ever before. Ethnology does no harm. All men are of one blood, it declares, in concert with the Scriptures.† War is deprecated as a cruel necessity, not gloried in as the proper work of man. It needs to be justified to the conscience of mankind. It never was attended by so many means of mitigating its horrors. How many chains our eyes have seen broken! Labor was never so much lightened. The miner is free and the factory child gets to school. Reformatories, asylums, prison-discipline, have superseded the hulks and Botany Bay.

This is to be noted by the preacher. Humanity, born of the Scripture, is to be brought up at its

---

* John viii. 36.   † Acts xvii. 26.

parent's knee, guided and directed. The clergy need not toil on every specific plan of benevolence, but they supply the fuel, and feed the flame of Christian compassion. They are commonly the wisest, best, and most disinterested friends of every beneficent agency, and they are so to bring Bible principles to bear, that weak sentimentalism or mechanical routine shall not supersede the true reforming agency, in the manifested love of God in Jesus Christ.

3. The Church is coming back to what she was before the age of Constantine, when civil power took her work too much in hand,—to what, in her purest portions, she was in the eighth, ninth, and tenth centuries. For it is historically true that as she was evangelical she was missionary; as she ceased to be evangelical she ceased to be evangelistic. The Reformation revived this zeal in both the Reformed and Roman Catholic communions; for no one who has not read and reflected estimates aright the extent to which the Reformation revived even the Church of Rome.

We must guide and maintain this missionary spirit by exhibiting the genius of Scripture, the uses of the Church, the lights of prophecy shining over so many dark places, the noble examples of saints, the true motives and means, the authoritative instructions of the Master, and the magnificence of the coming future. It is of little use to tell men to be good. The Gospel only shows us how enmity is exchanged for reconciliation, and how power to do good is given for the previous bondage to sin.

4. The yearning for Christian union is a favorable feature of our time. There are various ways of satisfying it—wise and foolish. The "Solemn League and Covenant" contemplated one method, of which the counterpart was tried on this continent. The English Government tried another way in making all civil officers communicants. It is a mark of the progress of opinion that we now see the folly and the mischief of such a plan. This spirit of union is to be directed from the pulpit. Denominationalism has its use; but we are to guard against its abuse. I have no notion of being cut off from that historic Christian Church, which was before the Papacy, and may be traced during the night of pre-Reformation times by the fires of persecution; nor from the Waldenses of Northern Italy; nor the Albigenses of Southern France; nor from Latimer, Ussher, Barrow, Butler, and

Leighton; nor from the Puritans of England in the national Church or out of it; nor from their descendants; nor from the Scottish believers—rugged like their native mountains, but firm like them; nor from Wesley and Whitfield; nor from Carey, and Andrew Fuller, and Robert Hall; nor from Oliver Cromwell, and Selden, and John Owen; nor, if you can show me successors in the Communion of Rome to Blaise Pascal, and Fenelon, and Thomas a Kempis, from them. They are of the family of which God is the Father, Jesus the elder Brother, and in which I claim membership. And I should count it indescribably base to glorify these mighty dead, now at the safe distance of heaven from me, and to ignore their representatives in the next parish, or look with jealousy or coldness on their successful labors.

The pulpit is to foster the spirit of union, which does not necessarily imply organic union, the effort after which may be only human pride striving for a great corporation, but which seeks co-operation, distribution of resources at home, and of laborers in foreign mission fields. Scripture direction, reproof and prediction are to be brought to bear on this, until as the Epistles to Romans, Corinthians, Galatians

Ephesians, and Philippians lie side by side in the blessed volume, all marked by individual features, yet all speaking the same language, breathing the same spirit, doing the same work, magnifying the same Lord, so the Churches of Jesus Christ shall be perfectly joined together, animated by one spirit, wasting no power on one another, but " steadfast and unmovable, always abounding in the work of the Lord." The Lord speed this most blessed era!

5. We should notice the practical character of our times. Mere theories and abstractions go for little. The idea that a minister's success lay in the number of persons whom he induced to take up his way, or hire his pews, is not now supreme.

Like the children in the lyric, as they saw the skulls turned up on Blenheim battle-field, and asked the details of the battle from the old man, who still put in the inquiry—

"But what good came of it, at last?"

so men most properly ask now, and will no more be satisfied than the children with the assurance that

"It was a famous victory."

Congregations must justify their existence. If they

only bring people together to be "very much pleased," why, the Lecture Bureaus will contract for all that. "Did you worship? Were you edified? Did the Lord speak to you? Did you speak to Him? Do you mean more seriously to be pure, honest, upright, generous, manly, holy, from what you did and heard to-day?" These are the questions which the best part of mankind feel to be proper, and to which we must have affirmative replies. All this is good for us, and should not be forgotten. The Bible is the most sensible book in the world. It has no dash of romance, no mixture of fanaticism, no flavor of a mutual admiration company. Its saints do not convene to purr over one another, but to instruct, help, and edify one another, and to influence the world. "By their fruits ye shall know them" is its axiom. "What fruit had ye in those things, of which ye are now ashamed?" is its fearless challenge to sinners. We, who preach, are to aim at visible saintship in ourselves and in our people, that this practical age may see that it is not a vain thing to serve the Lord.

6. It is, perhaps, a part of this practical element that we have so much so-called "Christian activity." The varied forms of it need not be specified. The

best impulses thereto, and the surest guidance therein, must come from the pulpit. We must help the people to discriminate between the energy of mere human flesh, which is fussy, self-asserting, self-conscious, easily provoked, easily discouraged, and the power of the spirit, which is quiet, gentle, meek, and, in a sense, indomitable.

We must put all service in its right place, not as a means toward acceptance, but as a blessed and cheerful fruit of it. "The Lord had respect to Abel and to his offering"—Abel first, then the offering. We must keep the eye of all Christian labor clear, single, looking right on.* "This I do, O Christ, for thee," we must keep up as its motto. If this principle cuts off some bazars, exhibitions, tableaux, and other fantastic ways of getting our money's worth of enjoyment, and crediting it to Christ, I do not think the Church will be much weaker.

We must keep up the standard of Christian living in the Christian laborer. Clean hands are needed to do Christian work. Character is before co-operation, being before doing. "Take heed unto thyself, and to the doctrine." †

---

* Prov. iv. 25. † 1 Tim. iv. 16.

Thus from the evil that we admit and deplore, but no less from the good for which we are glad and thankful, must we draw motives to zeal and fidelity, and receive aids to fitness as able ministers of the New Testament.

LECTURE X.

The idea is not to be conveyed by what is said of power to-day, that the pulpit has lost its force and usefulness. That impression is sometimes given out by literary men in the serials and magazines. Literary men, unhappily, as a rule, are not, and have not been, docile pupils of the pulpit. They have been apt to think of themselves as instructors of mankind; the editorial "we" beguiles them. They are not disposed, by their very professional life, to listen to men whose reliance is not on rhetoric, or the tricks of literary composition, but on truth unfamiliar to them, and on language simple and unadorned. There have been many noble exceptions, in men of high literary power and repute, with range of view wide enough to include the spiritual world, and with religious life sufficiently vigorous to crave and feed upon revealed truth. I speak of literary men as a class. They may be easily mistaken in their estimate; just as a corresponding error is indulged regarding oratory. You would suppose, to hear some men talk, that in the days of Philip of Macedon every man spoke like Demosthenes, and that every Roman politician expressed himself like Cicero. It is forgotten that it is the pre-eminence of Demosthenes over all his compeers that lifts him up to our view, that it is because Cicero was head-and-shoulders above his cotemporaries that he is an object of admiration to us. So it is with preachers. "Where," men say, " are the Summerfields and Whitfields?" It is to be borne in mind that they towered above their cotemporaries, that they were unapproached, and that in Whitfield's case, at least, he declared an unfamiliar gospel in a dead age. It would be reply enough to ask "Where were the Spurgeons, the Melvilles, the Robertsons, the Guthries, the Binneys, the Candlishes, the Paysons, the Kirks, the Alexanders, the Thornwells, of their time?" Or suppose the argument were applied to the press: where are the Horace Greeleys, the Raymonds, the Gordon Bennetts of the newspaper world? All gone—the press is effete, the newspapers not worth reading! These identical men, or copies of them, are not here.

There is infinite variety of gift, talent, and faculty; and the press, as a whole, is as able, fresh, and vigorous as it ever was. The same statement is emphatically true of the pulpit. You are not, gentlemen, going to a sinking profession. You fall into no forforn hope. You sacrifice yourselves to no lost cause. There never was more of energy, talent, zeal, culture, and ability consecrated to Christ in the pulpit than now, and you may catch a certain inspiration from the association with a noble, numerous, and devoted band of fellow-laborers, inferior to no race of ministers since the days of the apostles. I think there was as much piety, learning, and ability in the Council at New Haven as in the Council of Laodicea ; and the Evangelical Alliance Conference at New York, in 1873, would bear favorable comparison, for all that should distinguish the Christian ministry, with the Council of Nice. I would rather stand over Dean Alford than over Tertullian, Jonathan Edwards than Athenagoras, Charles Hodge than Jerome, and I prefer Moses Stuart of Andover to Clement of Alexandria.

If it be alleged that most sermons do not rise above mediocrity, let it be considered how many men at the bar, in the Senate, in the State Legislatures, rise above mediocrity. Make out a list of the noted orators of secular life in our own oratorical age, and it is not formidably lengthened.

What this final Lecture should be entitled is not very clear, but its object is to point out those elements of which we are to take note as combining to give weight and legitimate authority in pastoral work, and particularly in preaching. If some things are noticed on which you have not had occasion to think, do not on that account dismiss them; and if something be said which is familiar to you, regard it, please, as indication of the substantial identity of what I have been saying to you with the general instruction you have received here and elsewhere, and of the oneness of Christian brethren in conviction and in experience, though separated by form or organization.

1. There is a legitimate influence founded on official standing. Of course, if we had no other right to be respectfully heard; or if we paraded our license to preach with puerile and ridiculous vanity; or if we assumed, on the strength of it, airs which even as men and as gentlemen, we should not affect; or if, in virtue of being licensed and ordained, we walked

on stilts, spoke loftily, and otherwise displayed weakness and vanity, we should have slender claim to respectful hearing. It will be easy to instance such folly, to caricature it, and to swing round to the conclusion that there is no such thing as official standing.

But we assume ministers to have the average measure of taste, common sense, and modesty (if they lack these they should not be ministers); to be no more elated by their license than a physician by his diploma, or an officer by his commission; and no more reliant on the license for success than the doctor on his parchment or the officer on his uniform. To such a man there is a certain amount of influence derived from his official standing. That influence he carries to the pulpit. This may be inferred from the fact that the first ministers, meek and lowly as they were, do not fail to put their commission forward on all proper occasions. It is needless to quote the introductions to the epistles, many allusions in the body of the letters, and many arguments and appeals founded on their commission.* They were mes-

---

* See Acts x. 42; xx. 24; Rom. i. 1; xv. 16; 1 Cor. i. 1; iv. 1; 2 Cor. i. 1; iii. 6; iv. 1; xiii. 10; Gal. i. 1; Phil. i. 1, etc.; 1 Tim. i. 1, 12; 1 Pet. i. 1; v. 1.

sengers whose consequence depended on the Sender, embassadors whose position was fixed by the King they represented, and they were miraculously attested as sent of God. They never took pains to disclaim this official standing, or to denude themselves of any regard it might inspire. In all the sufferings, hardships, and perils of the time, they never shrink from the common lot of Christians. They will be as Jews to Jews, as Greeks to Greeks; they will make tents, beg money, minister to saints, do anything for their good; but it is as ministers of Jesus Christ. Not only so, but, if you will think of it, all self-renunciation, all condescension to men of low estate will be enhanced in its value by the distinct official position of those who enjoy the honor, but have none of the insolence of office.

And that men so understand it is proved by the whole machinery of associations, councils, presbyteries, or whatever other bodies recognize, set apart, or ordain. Why do they exist, if not to give such standing? and why give it, if it is worthless, and there is some merit in disclaiming every sign of it? In this regard we only carry out the plan of Scripture. There were some who had the rule, whoever they were, who were to be honored and obeyed. There were office-bearers, as distinguished from members, clothed with authority, according to Christ's laws, to administer the government of His house. That authority is not lordly, discretionary, nor legislative, but ministerial; that is, in submission to the word of the Master. They are not infallible; nor is their right to interpret the Divine Word exclusive. But the authority is real notwithstanding, however it may be regarded or limited; there is something in the position before the Church to which God calls a man through His Spirit, the Church having recognized that call.

Now, there seems to me no special wisdom in affecting to ignore all this, and reducing ourselves to the ranks. We are ministers of Jesus Christ, and we are to be careful that the office suffers no conspicuous dishonor through us. We have brethren in the ministry who stand to us in a different relation from that of ordinary believers, and it does not appear to me out of place here to urge you to the cultivation of a true brotherly feeling. Ministers ought to be able to sympathize with a minister better than laymen can do. We are bound to stand by our order, all the more from this, that the world is ready to judge ministers more severely than any other class. We are bound to strengthen each other with the people, to discourage querulous reports and gossip from them regarding their ministers, and to render mutual aid in difficulties and perplexities. We are to frown on the idea of rivalry, to scorn the policy of drawing members from our brethren.* We are to show, by cordial co-operation with brethren, that the cause of Jesus Christ is greater to us than individual interests, and to carry one another in prayer before the throne of our common Lord.

2. We have the power of educated mind. We are taught to set things in order, to make them clear, to illustrate truth, to present it persuasively and agreeably. We have advantages common to us with all educated speakers. These we are not to despise. God employs fitting instruments for the doing of His work. He said of Aaron: "I know that he can speak well." He sent on the Apostles tongues of fire.

---

* See an admirable paragraph on this subject in Vinet's *Pastoral Theology*, Fourth Part, ch. iii., on "Relations of Ecclesiastics among themselves."

Now, we have special education. We are trained to set forth the truth of God. We have studied the best modes of presenting it. We have not only general intelligence on this matter, but, when we stand up to preach, that particular sermon is the fruit of special study. You will, as you look over your audience, see many men who know much of which you are ignorant, who perhaps know moral or religious truth, as a whole, better than you do; who have wider general information, more varied observation, a quicker wit than yours; but you have gone to the store-house of truth, have made sure that you have a portion of it to give there and then, which you have mastered for that time, and of which, at the moment, you have more exact present knowledge than any of your hearers. This may give confidence and a certain sense of power in your speaking. Nor must it be forgotten that, as Schleiermacher tried to teach his countrymen, religion is not only in the region of knowing or in the region of doing, but of feeling and affection, assimilating the knowledge and stimulating to action. Nothing that has been said in these lectures is meant or, it is believed, fitted to depreciate vigorous mind or high education in the pulpit. The more of both we have in the service of Christ in His Church the better. But even ordinary average mind, thoroughly trained, can go about its proper work in preaching with the same kind of confidence with which ordinary average mind, professionally trained, does its work in the dispensary or the court-room.

3. We have the power of moral character. "For he was a good man, full of the Holy Ghost and of faith; and much people was added unto the Lord." * Is this collocation of phrases purely accidental? You are known to be sincere, disinterested, honest, desirous of doing good. You have lived and labored among the people. You remember Paul's appeal to the Thessalonians: "For our Gospel came not unto you in word only, but in power, and in the Holy Ghost, and in much assurance; as ye know what manner of men we were among you for your sake." † Let there be habitual emphasis on that element "for your sake." There is power from unselfish service—from living habitually before men's eyes a blameless, beneficent life. The man is felt to be greater than

---

* Acts xi. 24. † 1 Thess. i. 5.

what he says. It is a part of which he is the whole; and his personality is behind his speech. All the weight of him is with his words, as the force of a blow is measured in a gymnasium by, not that of the arm only, but also of the body that is behind the arm. So, gentlemen, when you are toiling in a community, looking up the lapsed, reclaiming the drunkard, persuading the careless to set up a family altar and make a true home, drawing children to the feet of Jesus, comforting the broken-hearted, helping tottering steps back into the ways of virtue and self-respect, mingling your tears with those of the miserable, or your gladness with the joys of the happy, praying with distracted parents by the cradle of their dying child—though you are not adding anything to your piles of manuscripts or your stores of book-learning, you are adding to the power with which the individual sermon goes to the hearts of the hearers.

It will be obvious that the acquisition of this moral power depends on the prosecution of ministerial labor in a right spirit; for obvious selfishness, vanity, self-seeking, petulance, impatience, and all such levity as the judgment of the people counts out of place, will seriously hinder its attainment.* The poor woman who, instead of replying to an impatient speech of her pastor, lifted up her hands and eyes and exclaimed, "Would to God I had never heard your voice but in the pulpit!" administered, all unconsciously, a rebuke which we must take care not to deserve. And if we are sometimes tired with half-comprehending, dull, perverse, or narrow good people, or by "unreasonable men," let us remember how much was endured by Him who became "a minister of the circumcision." Let us also bear in mind how often we, like the earliest Christian preachers, have been foolish, and slow-hearted in believing. And let us set over against the vexations the incidental favors which, in addition to the great reward in heaven, a most merciful and generous master throws in by the way, as we do the work of the ministry. How much confidence is given us! How much appreciation!

---

* And this will be a rule of action to ministers. In many instances they might, without injury to themselves, do or enjoy that which would "offend" the people. And in matters of mere personal gratification, a true minister will forego *rights*, because he is bent on *duties*. He will avoid that which, though to him indifferent or innocent, yet would raise a prejudice against his message.

How often, when we are despising ourselves for miserable preaching, some true child of God comes and, half-ashamed to intrude, says, It has done me so much good! How many prayers go up for us from aged disciples, young converts, and little children! How much more human affection we enjoy than we deserve! When a fellow-laborer of mine died, who had no cares but his parish, and not much to recommend him but his ministerial devotedness, a poor waitress, a member in his church, said to me, with sobs and tears, "I loved him—next to my own father—the best in all the world." It is worth much to have the grateful regard of true hearts, however lowly.

4. We have the power of the word of God. What He makes has perfect fitness for its end. All the world is adapted to man. Hence we construct our argument for the unity (not necessarily the *unicity*, or numerical oneness, but the unity, which implies plurality) of God. He who made the cattle made the grass which is fitted to them, as they are to man. But the maker of the grass is maker of the seasons on which it is dependent. But the seasons depend on the earth's movements, and it on the arrangements

of the solar system; so one plan runs through all, and one divine mind arranged and completed the whole complicated system. Now, if all the parts of the universe be fitted for their uses, it is fair to conclude that the same is true of His word which He has so much magnified. Let us believe in it as perfectly adapted to the objects of our ministry.

It is easy, indeed, to trace the progress of revelation, the influences that formed the mind of prophets and apostles, the chances to which manuscripts and versions have been exposed, the variety of "readings," and the human features which the book, by its very nature, wears. One may so pertinaciously dwell on all these, that it shall seem to him as not very different from a good human book. Thus men have so exclusively dwelt on the human experiences of our Saviour's life, His birth and growth, His hunger, thirst, weariness, dying, and His expressions of what was true of Him as man, that they have ignored His divine nature and eternal existence. Now the word written is like the Word incarnate—it has a human and a divine side, and we must not, in studying its lower, lose sight of its higher, nature. It is "quick and powerful, sharper than any two-edged sword."

(Heb iv. 12.) Let us have confidence in it. Let us take "the sword of the Spirit which is the word of God." (Eph. vi. 12.) The military officer having had his sword ground and sharpened for the campaign—a preparation such as your studies here are meant to give you—does not wrap it around with flowers, or ribbons. That were childish. Nor must we lessen the power of the word to cut and penetrate, by wrapping it in our poetry, speculation, and philosophy. Let it—itself—with its two edges reach the soul and spirit. It will discern "the thoughts of the heart." Men will think some one reported their cases to us, as the word lays them bare. They will say "That was for me;" for it is powerful to awaken, to reveal, to cast down imaginations, to expose refuges of lies, to convince of sin, to cheer, to comfort, to stimulate, to sanctify.

Let us preach the law for evangelical purposes, that men, judged and condemned of their own consciences and coming to God in Christ, may escape being condemned of Him. Let us so preach the Gospel that we shall magnify the law, and establish it. Divine mercy is not a grave in which Justice is buried out of sight; nor is Jesus a milder divinity who propitiates a stern avenger. God so loved the world that He gave Jesus Christ—"that whosoever believeth in Him should not perish but have eternal life." "Yea, we establish the law." Christ, in making atonement, is the exponent and expression of Eternal Love. His cross is, at the same time, the mightiest contribution to the majesty of law the world has ever seen. In Him God is just, and yet the justifier of the believer.

Let us be evangelical, like Paul, Peter, and John. Let us be ethical, like James; and, if we catch the spirit of all, we shall feel and exhibit no real contradiction. We shall see Paul and James, two disciples going on their Master's business, when they are assailed before and behind. Self-righteousness is faced by Paul. "By the deeds of the law shall no flesh be justified." "A man is justified by faith without the deeds of the law."* These are his blows at the enemy to whom he is opposed. Licentiousness, in whatever form it perverts grace into a cover for sin, has to be grappled with by James. "O, vain

---

* Rom. iii., 20, 28. It was not, surely, a mere accident that this demonstration should have been made "to all that be in Rome."

man! faith without works is dead." "By works a man is justified, and not by faith only."* These are *his* blows at his foe. Do not be afraid. He is not striking at Paul, nor Paul at him. They are not foes, but friends, as Arnot somewhere puts it, "back to back." Each has his own foe, and each is fighting his single combat; but they are on the same side. "The battle is the Lord's." And if we set forth the same truths in the same connections we shall, possibly, be charged with inconsistency, but the desired result will be reached, and our hearers will be "doers of the word and not hearers only."

Have we not seen how often men of rude speech and narrow mind, with little grace of manner, often with glaring faults of thought and reasoning, great deficiency in taste, and even a spice of egotism, have yet preached the great leading truths of the Gospel in Gospel language, and with most blessed spiritual results? We do not forbid these men, "lay preachers,"

---

* James ii. 20, 24. The more eagerly and vehemently we set forth in the free Gospel of God's grace a righteousness which we no more work out than we make the sun, the more urgently should we press on men that the true acceptance of Jesus as Priest is also acceptance of Him as King. Loose living among professing Christians is a sad foe to the doctrines of grace.

"evangelists," or whatever else they may be called, because in our judgment they are unscientific in thought and inconsecutive in speech. We are glad of their results. When the New England farmers settled on the prairies of Illinois, and found the fever and ague disputing their possession of the place, they acquired enough medical skill to carry—like Livingstone in the African swamps—the store of quinine, and to use it perhaps with some disregard of the precision of pharmacy. And even so, the friends who set forth the Gospel of God's grace, with some violations of theological proprieties, yet do good—sometimes where they do not know, or even expect it— and their success is one more admonition to us to wield the same weapon, or, changing the figure, to exhibit the same remedy. Even when we have to reason and argue, the most cogent and convincing proofs we can bring to our audiences will be from the Word of God. It is powerful to refute and convince.*

---

* "In general," says Dr. Broadus, "rely mainly on Scriptural arguments, and prefer those which are plain and unquestionable." A TREATISE ON THE PREPARATION AND DELIVERY OF SERMONS, by JOHN A. BROADUS, D.D., LL.D., Professor in the

5. There is a power we legitimately acquire by laying bare, from the Word, man's wants, and offering a suitable remedy. Men need to be converted, brought to peace, rest, assurance.

After the fashion of our blessed Lord,* of his apostles,† after the fashion of the Reformers of the sixteenth century, of the Puritan preachers, of the Reformers of the last century—Whitfield, Wesley, and their associates—let us, through that Word which is given for this very thing, seek the conversion of men, directly, immediately, constantly.

For consider what is their attitude. God is the one supreme object worthy of affection, trust, obedience. He is fixed, abiding, immutable. He is a fountain always full and for all, a sun always shining. But some are not looking to Him at all. They need to be converted—turned to look at Him. Some are serving dumb idols—they need to be

---

Southern Baptist Seminary, Greenville, S. C. This volume is marked particularly by fullness, minuteness, and the force of "good sense." It augurs well for the future ministry of our Baptist brethren that they are receiving training like that of this book, which only came under the author's notice, he regrets to say, when most of these lectures had been written.

* Matt. xviii. 3. † Acts iii. 19.

turned to Him, and from them. Some have heard of Him, and are deliberately turning their backs on Him, rejecting Him, saying to Him: "What have I to do with Thee?" They need to be converted. And some who have turned and looked to Him are looking away, or trying to look at once to Him and to other objects, of ambition, or indulgence, or selfishness, or worldliness. They need, like Peter, to be "converted"—reconverted, restored; and the means are the same as in the case of the others, and the process through which they must pass is not essentially different. They, too, must repent, and do the first works. There is not an open, common way by which sinners come to the mercy-seat, and a retired and private way for backsliding saints. If disciples go back into the ways of sinners, as sinners they must weep bitterly and be forgiven and restored.

And if men are thus alienated from God, how cogent are the reasons for our seeking, by the means He gives us, their conversion, seeing that in a way that must remain a mystery to us here, it pleases God to employ human instrumentality for saving purposes. Remember the doom of unbelief: "I called and ye refused. I stretched out my hand and no man regarded." Remember the words from the lips of Incarnate mercy, "Depart ye cursed!" Remember the solemn and judicial statement, "He that hath not the Son shall not see life; but the wrath of God abideth on him." Nor can we forget the danger of those who, without apparent deliberate rejection of God's overtures, practically disregard them. "How shall we escape if we neglect so great salvation?" Could its utter impossibility be more forcibly suggested than by the unanswerable question? That there was intelligence only aggravates the guilt, and intensifies the doom. I know how some, bending, I must think, the principles of exegesis to their feelings of humanity, substitute "end of being" for punishment; but we cannot well read that the servant who knew his lord's will and did it not shall be annihilated, where the master says "beaten with many stripes." There are no degrees in annihilation. We are not informed—for the Scriptures are practical, and never make a needless parade of knowledge—regarding them who never heard the way of life; but to us the appeal may well be made: "He that despised

Moses' law died without mercy under two or three witnesses: of how much sorer punishment, suppose ye, shall he be thought worthy, who hath trodden under foot the Son of God, and hath counted the blood of the covenant, wherewith he was sanctified, an unholy thing, and hath done despite unto the Spirit of grace? For we know him that hath said, Vengeance belongeth unto me, I will recompense, saith the Lord. And again, The Lord shall judge his people. It is a fearful thing to fall into the hands of the living God."

It may seem to some as if this put the Lord in an unfavorable light; but we are no judges of such matters. It is our own cause. Probably some of the juvenile criminals in our prisons regard the laws that keep them there unfavorably. But that, surely, is no reason for changing the laws. Their views can neither be candid nor comprehensive; and the chasm between them and virtuous citizens is nothing to the great gulf fixed between the Lord God Omnipotent and human criminals. *

---

* It is alleged, indeed, that figurative language is confessedly employed in the descriptions of the future of the impenitent, and the question is put to the popular mind—Shall there be

But that the Scriptural view of God's anger against impenitent man robs God of His majesty is a chimera. If it has ever had this effect, it is because the presentation has been incomplete. The "severity" has been detached from the "goodness."

For another reason for our seeking the conversion of men is found in God's manifested love and mercy in Christ. He has sent His Son. The atonement has been made. All things are ready. His hands are stretched out in entreaty. His voice calls men to the mercy-seat: "This is my beloved Son, hear ye him." His Son left behind him the means of reaching and inviting the race: any limit put to the giving of this invitation is the work of man, not of God. His servants they "took, and beat one, and killed another." Yet he continues to send them. His Spirit pleads in human consciences—all too often in vain. What man is there able to assert the

---

literal fire and brimstone? But what then? Shall there be literal streets of pure gold like clear glass? This, too, is figurative; but does it prove that there is no heaven? Why do men use figures? Because they mean nothing? Or is it not because common didactic speech fails to convey the force and vividness of the intended idea? Figures without any basis of fact would be falsehoods.

silence of a voice within him? But it speaks innumerable warnings in vain. Imagination, lust, love of pleasure, or ease, or money, or power, make their reports to the Will, and, affecting sometimes a great show of fairness and deliberation, it decides against Conscience so uniformly that the wounded and discouraged monitor retires to write those records of contemptuous refusal that shall be read in the light of the judgment day.

Let me implore you, then, dear friends, if it please God to put you into the ministry, prepare your sermons from the Word, and order your work with a view to the conversion of men. That they be intelligent, orderly, cultured, is well. That they be converted is the consummation short of which it is not permitted to you to stay your efforts. Labor to "present every man perfect in the day of Christ." Tell them that they lose by every day they stay away from the Saviour, even if they be saved at last. Tell them that every day's delay diminishes the likelihood of their turning to the Lord, for the heart grows accustomed to evil, and the will takes its set; tell them that every day's resistance to the Spirit increases the likelihood of the Spirit's withdrawal. Tell them that while death's arrows are in every wind, they run positive risk of death eternal. Do not fear men's frowns. None will reproach you for fidelity in the day of accounts—none on their deathbeds. Do not fear the alleged "current of opinion." It was thus that Edwards, Brainard, Dwight, and Payson, preached, and the noblest and most enduring things in New England were the result. If the sentiment of the time is against their way, so much the worse for the sentiment! Paul and Peter and John and James so "reproved and rebuked and exhorted, with all long-suffering and doctrine." Nor is this New Testament doctrine only. That men turn to the Lord has been the one imperative demand of all Scripture: "Turn ye, turn ye, why will ye die?" The one unanswerable appeal from Divine mercy, and the one way of reconciliation and sonship, from the first, has been to Jew and Gentile, as the Lord said by Jeremiah (xxiv. 7): "And I will give them an heart to know me, that I am the Lord: and they shall be my people, and I will be their God: *for they shall return unto me with their whole heart.*"

6. And, finally, there is available the power of the Holy Ghost. He came on the early prophets and their words became oracles; on the Son of Man,* and He spake with authority; on the early disciples, and they spake as with tongues of fire.

There are, indeed, conditions of His coming, for God gives His gifts in a way appropriate to their nature and to that of their recipients. *Prayer* is one of these, easy in appearance, difficult in reality to our proud nature. Most men will find it easier to preach than to pray in secret.

Renunciation of our own strength is implied. We must be emptied of self, that we may be filled with the spirit. The tradition still lingers in the place, after two centuries, of a historical sermon. A young minister was desired to preach on the "Communion-Monday," as is called, in Scotland and Ireland, the day after the Lord's Supper has been observed. He trembled, went to the fields, tried to evade the duty, was brought almost by violence: and five hundred souls dated their spiritual impressions from the sermon. Strength was perfected in felt weakness.

---

* See Isa. lxi., and Luke iv. 18.

Hard work is implied; not our indolence or ease, but labor, is the channel in which the divine energy flows. We must labor in getting possession of the truth, in telling it, and in following up our public teaching by private effort. The lesson taught by Quintilian, and ascribed to many others, we must learn; bottles must have the water—not thrown on them standing in rows, but—poured into each, one by one, if they are to be filled.

There must be *a single eye*. It would not be safe to trust success in the hands of the proud and self-seeking. They would claim the glory and be made worse.

There must be *true love;* to the good our superiors as generous admiration, to our equals as brotherly affection, to the vile and wicked as compassion. Love lays the wires along which the fire runs. Hearts burning with hate drive away the gentle dew. Shall the Holy Dove come down, great as the need is, where anger, wrath, malice, and envy make a church their arena? But where the Spirit comes the feeblest worker, for spiritual purposes, is irresistible.

But what shall we say more—what can we say more—than our Lord said to His disciples? "He that believeth on me, the works that I do shall he do also." What! unstop deaf ears, open blind eyes, raise the dead? Yes; even so, nor is this all: "And greater works than these shall he do, because I go to my Father." (John xiv. 12.) Greater! Yes; even so. "Greater" in numbers, in their diffusion, in their startling accompaniments—even the shadow of Peter healing—and in the results over the pagan world. But they did them in Him, as His; by His Spirit, for He fails not to say, "Because I go to my Father." He sends the Spirit down, and such results follow as Peter's sermon produced.

Oh! for this Spirit of truth, light, love, holiness, on colleges and seminaries, on ministers and missionaries, on churches, and Christless hearers! Without Him, we are going through the motions of God's army, but winning few conquests. With Him, we become a victorious host. The people fall under Him. He rules in the midst of His enemies. "Gird thy sword upon thy thigh, O most mighty, with thy glory and thy majesty. And in thy majesty ride prosperously, because (in the cause) of truth, and meekness, and righteousness."

APPENDIX.

(*Various questions having been put in writing, a separate hour was devoted to their consideration. Questions and answers are here given, omitting only those which have no general interest. Sometimes one paper contained more than one query.*)

Would it not aid a minister, on entering a new parish, to obtain, at the first, the roll of members of the church, so as to know who they are?

I can hardly think of a minister overlooking this matter at the very outset; and if he did overlook it, I should hope deacons or elders would make the suggestion. If they do not work themselves, they ought surely to be a kind of external conscience to the pastor.

In making the acquaintance of the people, in the first pastoral calls, is it best to avoid speaking on religious topics, unless they are suggested by the other parties; and to make the acquaintance of the people before speaking on such topics in pastoral calls?

Much will depend on circumstances. If, for example, your congregation is such that you call once in every couple of months, as many can, you may defer direct introduction of religious topics.

So also if you are being taken round to be introduced. But if you have a large congregation, and once a year is almost as much as you can hope to see the families, then it is too long to defer the business of your visit till some time in the second year of your pastorate.

Then, again, discrimination must be made, founded on the *kind* of the families and individuals. Some are demonstrative; others, no less true and good, shrink from the expression of their own spiritual feelings.

One rule is safe: let all the talking with the members of the congregation on religion be about their own, and not their neighbors' religion. Many persons fluently confess the sins of their former pastors, and those of their fellow-worshipers. Do not hear such confessions, if you can help it.

Ought *every* sermon have Christ for the focus?

Every sermon ought to have the doctrine of Christ in it in form or in solution. One may preach Christ controversially, non-evangelically; and one may preach law, commandments, duties, evangelically. In a congregation that is large, frequented by strangers, with many non-communicants, I should like to put a distinct word for Christ in every address. Nor need this be monotonous, for He is offered to men in endless variety of ways.

<small>Is it well to follow any system or round of doctrine in preaching?</small>

It is well to be consecutive. Imagine the sermons of Dwight's Theology preached without regard to subject, and their diminished value to intelligent hearers. If it is meant to follow in one's own mind any system, I do not see how an orderly mind can help it. One is as much bound by the laws of thought to have a system of doctrine as a botanist to have a system of botany. He sees a plant, and cannot help thinking where it belongs. So a theologian feels regarding a truth. Truths are in families as much as plants, and like human families in this, that if you know one member well you cannot well help getting introduced to the others.

<small>How shall we reach the masses? Will not free-seat system, by abolishing class distinction, help to solve this problem?</small>

I have no expectations from the "free-seat" system. It is, in my judgment, a product of sentiment and ignorance of human nature. The masses are to be reached as leaven reaches the masses of dough. It infects the particles next it, and they the next, and so on. I should hope much from churches so constructed that the poorest householders could also be pewholders. Giving money to support religion is a part of a religious education.

How do you make prayer-meetings interesting?

This whole subject is mixed up. "Interesting" to whom? The Lord? The suppliants? The spectators? The only way is to teach men to pray; to eliminate those who preach, or rhapsodize, or scold, or "lament," interminably; to promote general fervor among the people, and apply to the meeting the ordinary principles of Christian common sense. I would not set much store by "interesting" prayer-meetings by themselves. I have known of such that were little more than a young people's frolic. The prayer-meeting will be as the taste and as the life of the congregation.

Please say something about choosing a field. At home or abroad? East or West?

No one can give general directions here of any value. A man with no facility for learning new tongues should not go to a foreign field. A man whose nature is not elastic, who is offended with new things, ought not to go West. One must con-

ABOUT THE SINGING. 263

sider his own aptitudes; and when he has done his best to reach a conclusion, he may find himself where he never thought he was fit for. A man must put himself at his Master's disposal, and be ready to go where the way seems open. It is a nice thing when the field chooses him.

What is your opinion of the plan, which has been adopted in some places, of substituting a *Bible-exercise* for the second sermon on Sunday?

If we got parishes, like handfuls of dough, to be molded as we please, a Bible-exercise might be a good second service; but we do not. There are the "traditions of the elders," and violent dealing with them and the alienation of good people more than outweigh the good. Here and there "Bible-exercises," while fresh, or in the hands of versatile men, do much; but there is often a drawback. Get up Bible-classes. Teach them yourself. Get others to teach them, and make your second sermon a good Bible-exercise. We must teach the people as they are able to bear it.

Do you include choir singing among the fine arts which are *not* of assistance to the preacher of the gospel?

Whenever singing is so elaborate that the people

cannot join, it is an evil; and it matters little whether the evil is from solo, quartette, or choir. And if the whole congregation came to sing so that the attention would be largely fixed *on the singing*, it would be an evil too. Everybody laughs at the story of "the most eloquent prayer ever addressed to the people of Boston." There is the same underlying absurdity to me in the praise of God being "grand." Grand to whom? (See Ps. li. 17 and Isa. lxvi. 1, 2.)

It has appeared to me that the ministrations of the pastor to the sick are often hurtful to the work of the physician. For instance, the favorable issue of a certain case, the doctor is assured, depends almost entirely upon quietness and absence of things that would bring excitement. The pastor, in his kind consolation, speaks of future hopes, which will immediately convey to the mind of the sick person the idea that his is considered a doubtful case. This, unless the person is already well resigned, and, perhaps, then, will bring more or less of excitement, which may be damaging.

This will, perhaps, indicate what is meant. Will you please give us some suggestions upon this matter? And, as a result of your experience, how far, do you conclude, the pastor should, as a matter of discretion as well as courtesy, commit himself to the directions of the physician, as to when and how far these things should be spoken of?

Physicians are like other men—wise and otherwise; but they are physicians, and when a man puts himself, or is placed by his friends, in a physician's hands, the physician is master at his own discretion. I may have reason to think a parishioner is trusting his affairs in the hands of a lawyer of defective wisdom or integrity, but I have no right and no call, unless consulted, to urge my opinion on my parishioner. So, if the doctor says his patient is to see no one, I have no call to go. It is a part of a man's liberty, as regards me, to trust his money in the hands of anybody, and to commit himself to a doctor absolutely; and in the case described I have no responsibility. Practically, I have had no difficulty with medical men. It will usually be found that where they say a visit is useless, on account of the mental condition of the patient, they are right.

At the same time, I think doctors sometimes mistake as to the effect of a prayer, for example. Men are as often soothed and quieted as disturbed by religious truth. Of course a minister should have common sense in his visits. But that is an element which neither profession can secure in the members of the other.

And it does seem to me absurd, in a Christian country, perhaps family, for a man, about whose relation to God and eternity nothing is known, to be kept in the doctor's hands till there is not a hope for his life—till, perhaps, his brain is wandering or he is comatose—and then call the clergyman. But the trouble is that so many are keenly solicitous about getting human care for the body, and so willing to run risks in a world where loss or safety is not cognizable. I remember a bright woman, a physician's daughter, mentioning to me that a medical man had been brought to see a gentleman, whose fee exceeded the annual income of the patient's clergyman. "Well," said she, "it shows how much more men think of their bodies than their souls." It was not logical, but it had a basis of fact.

Suppose a missionary of the Mormon Church (or, as he would call it, of the "Reorganized Church of Jesus Christ of Latter Day Saints") comes into a town and plants a church, what is the duty of the ministers of other churches in town, and what their wisest course?

I am interested in this, because such a church has lately been planted in the town where I live, and may be, I suppose, in any other town.

One must consider the circumstances. Ministers may advertise obscure errors into notoriety or apparent importance. The circulation of a terse and timely tract, the use of a newspaper column, or the lesson in the Bible-class, may warn, or, better still, pre-occupy with the opposed truth. Not that I have any fear of controversy honestly and ably conducted. But it must have an adequate and good purpose. I heard, the other day, of a minister who always got into controversial preaching when the warm weather made people drowsy. He kept them listening by showing up the rival denominations.

I would like to ask about the experience of a minister. What relation should his preaching bear to his experience?

One who honestly expounds God's word will often set forth experiences he may not have: if, for example, he expounds the Ephesians. But he will set them forth as Paul's. If he has no rapturous feelings of his own he will not speak—if he is perfectly truthful—as if he had just been in the third heavens. A preacher ought to avoid every falsetto note. When he can say "I know this, from experience, to be true," let him say it.

If I have rightly understood an illustration given in your lecture on February 26, you fully recognize the fact that inactivity not only tends to paralyze the inactive members of the body, but also to enfeeble the other members.

Is it not, then, the duty of a Christian minister to insist upon, that the Christian women should take an active part in prayer-meetings?

Does not the silence of the women tend to diminish the activity of the male members of the church? And does it not produce much of that dragging and dullness which is so prevalent in prayer-meetings?

Inactivity of a Church where *it ought to be active* is paralysis, and a paralyzed man, unable to take exercise, gets other maladies. An idle Church gets fatty degeneration of the heart; or it gets to be censorious, quarrelsome, or something undesirable. But this argument vailed under a question, *begs the question.* My statement had respect to neglected duty. It assumes that it is the duty of Christian women to take an active part in mixed meetings. But that is in dispute. Whether women's active aid, as speakers or leaders, would improve the prayer-meeting, as such, I cannot tell. I think it would make them more "lively" sometimes. I am strongly in favor of women's prayer-meetings; and the most of the good Christian women I know would rather attend a dull mixed meeting than lead it in prayer. But I do not judge the excellent persons who think otherwise.

About what proportion of a pastor's time should be devoted to pastoral work, and how much to his studies?

I think a minister in good health, and doing his

work easily and naturally, should visit some on at least five days of every week. I have done that for months together, and would do it now if it were not for interminable boards, committees, and other distractions of which the Millennial Church will be free. A few hours a day spent in visiting give exercise, bodily, intellectual, moral. One studies better for it. "Are there not twelve hours in the day?" Each man must determine how much is to be given to study; only let him not call it study when he is lying on the sofa, laughing over "*The Innocents Abroad*."

How can a minister find out what is the best literature of the day, and how can he most easily and effectually keep up with the most advanced knowledge of the day in connection with his regular duties?

A good review, the talk of his brethren, and a clerical club, ought to keep him acquainted with good books. It is a great snare to many men to be abreast of the literature of the time. What does a parish in Maine care about the writer of Shakespeare, or the author of Junius' Letters?

In our country towns, probably, not half of the population attend churches. How, or by what measures, can this outside population be effectually reached?

Preach so that those who attend will report favorably, and then go to the houses of the non-attendants and confirm the report. I have labored for five years to get persons to church, and been rewarded with success. Our people could help us in that effort if they would.

Have you any opinion regarding clerical smoking?

Yes, a very unfavorable opinion. I was brought up to think badly of it; so you may discount my view. But I cannot but think that the flavor of smoking is offensive to many delicate persons, and it is difficult to many to smoke and lack some odor of it. Many "nice" people, even though some of their own family smoke, dislike it in ministers. I think it often injurious and not often necessary, and would advise those who have not become dependent on tobacco to preserve their freedom.

Is any account to be made of clerical manners?

Undoubtedly: a clergyman has no more right to be rude, slovenly, or ill-bred, than any other gentleman. He may be ignorant of some of the forms of artificial society; but he will be forgiven if he has obviously gentle feeling. No minister ought to take liberties because he is a minister.

Should there be devotional exercises at every pastoral visit?

Not necessarily; company, interruptions, or occupation of the family may render reading or prayer, or both, undesirable. But a minister should make his people understand that he is always happy to be invited: and as far as possible, he should encourage the people to admit him to the living room. How much time city ministers lose in looking at drawing-room furniture!

Would it be wise for a minister to give selections, occasionally, to his people, instead of his own?

Perhaps so. But he should announce them as selections. That is demanded by honesty; and soon the people would feel that they could select for themselves, and want another minister.

What relation should the text bear to the sermon?

The text should sustain, suggest, and give tone to the sermon. The main thought of the text should usually be the main thought of the sermon. A text must not be made a *pretext*.

In *delivering* your sermons, to what extent do you recall the *language* in which they were *written ?*

When you have once put a thought into the best language you know, and have to repeat the thought, the mind will readily run in the same track, and without effort. But no attempt is made to recall the language, except where something turns on a word. In point of fact, only a small proportion of the phraseology is reproduced. No effort should be made to remember structure of sentences, or collocations of phrases, or even place of paragraphs. If a paragraph does not come in naturally, let it go.

Should the writing of a sermon be commenced before all the material is collected and orderly arranged ?

I think it is better to be in possession of enough materials, and an arrangement, before you begin the final writing. You may leave out some of your material, and find new and better, as you advance. But it is wise to have enough at the beginning. Most ministers have pieces of sermons that never got themselves finished—"untimely figs," of no use to any human interest.

Should a minister entirely avoid theatrical and operatic performances ?

I am a poor authority on this. I never saw a play acted; never was at the opera in my life.

I presume there is a difference between the two. I find ministers speaking on both sides of the theater question in the same sermon. All the evidence I have yet seen is to the effect that—whatever its abstract powers might be—the theater is, in point of fact, mischievous on the whole. The best evidence of its effect is that the pure plays cannot get players or spectators. Those of Shakespeare are, it is alleged, kept on the stage at a ruinous cost. The average play-goer must have his moral teaching at the theater highly spiced, and increasingly so from year to year. So I never go, never advise any one to go, am sorry when I hear of Christians going, and think a minister's usefulness in danger from going.

Many say that a minister should never speak to a female alone. What is wise on that subject?

Such a rule is absurd and impossible in practice. No minister ever held to it. Much nonsense has been talked and written, especially lately, on this subject. I have seen articles in religious papers that were a libel on the Christian Church; as if Christian women,

Trieste

Trieste Publishing has a massive catalogue of classic book titles. Our aim is to provide readers with the highest quality reproductions of fiction and non-fiction literature that has stood the test of time. The many thousands of books in our collection have been sourced from libraries and private collections around the world.

The titles that Trieste Publishing has chosen to be part of the collection have been scanned to simulate the original. Our readers see the books the same way that their first readers did decades or a hundred or more years ago. Books from that period are often spoiled by imperfections that did not exist in the original. Imperfections could be in the form of blurred text, photographs, or missing pages. It is highly unlikely that this would occur with one of our books. Our extensive quality control ensures that the readers of Trieste Publishing's books will be delighted with their purchase. Our staff has thoroughly reviewed every page of all the books in the collection, repairing, or if necessary, rejecting titles that are not of the highest quality. This process ensures that the reader of one of Trieste Publishing's titles receives a volume that faithfully reproduces the original, and to the maximum degree possible, gives them the experience of owning the original work.

We pride ourselves on not only creating a pathway to an extensive reservoir of books of the finest quality, but also providing value to every one of our readers. Generally, Trieste books are purchased singly - on demand, however they may also be purchased in bulk. Readers interested in bulk purchases are invited to contact us directly to enquire about our tailored bulk rates. Email: customerservice@triestepublishing.com

You May Also Like

The Credibility of the Christian Religion; Or, Thoughts on Modern Rationalism

Samuel Smith

ISBN: 9780649557516
Paperback: 204 pages
Dimensions: 5.83 x 0.43 x 8.27 inches
Language: eng

On Spermatorrhœa: Its Pathology, Results, and Complications

J. L. Milton

ISBN: 9780649663057
Paperback: 188 pages
Dimensions: 6.14 x 0.40 x 9.21 inches
Language: eng

www.triestepublishing.com

You May Also Like

Hour by Hour; Or, The Christian's Daily Life

E. A. L.

ISBN: 9780649607242
Paperback: 172 pages
Dimensions: 6.14 x 0.37 x 9.21 inches
Language: eng

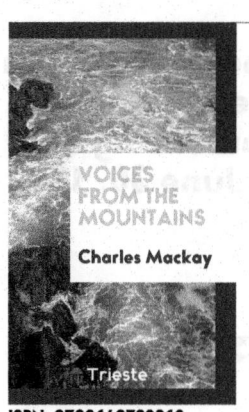

Voices from the Mountains

Charles Mackay

ISBN: 9780649730360
Paperback: 140 pages
Dimensions: 5.25 x 0.30 x 8.0 inches
Language: eng

www.triestepublishing.com

You May Also Like

1807-1907 The One Hundredth Anniversary of the incorporation of the Town of Arlington Massachusetts

Various

ISBN: 9780649420544
Paperback: 108 pages
Dimensions: 6.14 x 0.22 x 9.21 inches
Language: eng

Biennial report of the Board of State Harbor Commissioners, for the two fiscal years commencing July 1, 1890, and ending June 30, 1892

Various

ISBN: 9780649194292
Paperback: 44 pages
Dimensions: 6.14 x 0.09 x 9.21 inches
Language: eng

www.triestepublishing.com

You May Also Like

Biennial report of the Board of State Harbor Commissioners for the two fisca years. Commeneing July 1, 1884, and Ending June 30, 1886

Various

ISBN: 9780649199693
Paperback: 48 pages
Dimensions: 6.14 x 0.10 x 9.21 inches
Language: eng

Biennial report of the Board of state commissioners, for the two fiscal years, commencing July 1, 1890, and ending June 30, 1892

Various

ISBN: 9780649196395
Paperback: 44 pages
Dimensions: 6.14 x 0.09 x 9.21 inches
Language: eng

Find more of our titles on our website. We have a selection of thousands of titles that will interest you. Please visit

www.triestepublishing.com

Lightning Source UK Ltd.
Milton Keynes UK
UKOW06f1113231017
311488UK00006B/1268/P